PILGRIM ROAD

A BENEDICTINE JOURNEY
THROUGH LENT

Albert Holtz, O.S.B.
Illustrations by the author

MOREHOUSE PUBLISHING

Harrisburg – New York

Unless otherwise noted, the Scripture quotations contained herein are from the New Revised Standard Version Bible, copyright © 1989 by the Division of Christian Education of the National Council of Churches of Christ in the U.S.A. Used by permission. All rights reserved.

Quotations from the *Rule of Benedict* so designated are from *RB1980: The Rule of Benedict in English* (Collegeville, Minn.: The Liturgical Press, 1981). Permission granted by the Liturgical Press.

Most of the stories in this book originally appeared in a slightly altered form in *A Saint on Every Corner: Glimpses of Holiness Beyond the Monastery* by Albert Holtz, O.S.B. (Notre Dame, IN: Ave Maria Press, 1998).

Morehouse Publishing, P.O. Box 1321, Harrisburg, PA 17105

Morehouse Publishing, 445 Fifth Avenue, New York, NY 10016

Morehouse Publishing is an imprint of Church Publishing Incorporated.

Cover art by Dorothy Thompson Perez

Cover design by Brenda Klinger

Library of Congress Cataloging-in-Publication Data

Holtz, Albert.
  Pilgrim road : a Benedictine journey through Lent / Albert Holtz.
  p. cm.
  ISBN-13: 978-0-8192-2251-0 (pbk.)
  1. Lent—Meditations. 2. Benedict, Saint, Abbot of Monte Cassino.
3. Benedictines—Spiritual life. I. Title.
BV85.H65 2006
242'.34—dc22
                                                              2006029585

Printed in the United States of America

07 08 09 10 11   10 9 8 7 6 5 4 3 2

CONTENTS

INTRODUCTION

The image of life as a journey comes to mind so easily that it must have occurred to the very first people who reflected on the meaning of human existence. Certainly Christian tradition has always been fond of the metaphor of the earthly journey toward the heavenly Jerusalem. This book celebrates four different kinds of journey.

The Christian Pilgrimage

The custom of making a pilgrimage to a shrine or holy place is found in all major religions, and has been part of Christian tradition since the early 200s. In the middle ages, long before modern transportation, millions of Christian pilgrims endured grim hardships and physical dangers on their journeys to holy places to fulfil some pilgrim vow, to ask a favor, or to give thanks. Among the hundreds of Christian pilgrimage sites, the most important were Jerusalem, Rome, and Santiago de Compostela in Spain. A trip to one of these places could take months or even years, and would often leave the returning pilgrim changed forever.

The Lenten Journey

The forty days of Lent symbolize the forty days that Jesus spent fasting and praying in the desert. But that number forty was, in turn, meant to remind us of the forty years that the Israelites spent in the desert. The Church has always seen in the Israelite's journey from Egypt to the Promised Land, from bondage to liberation, an apt image of the Christian's Lenten journey from Ash Wednesday to Easter.

The Inward Journey

We Christians are called to journey with Christ into the innermost truth about ourselves, meeting on the way all of our brokenness and imperfections, but finding at our center the Holy and Living God. The inward pilgrimage of conversion is the most important voyage any of us ever takes. The traditional Lenten disciplines of self-denial, almsgiving, and prayer are, therefore, not ends in themselves, but are always at the service of this inward journey.

The Sabbatical Trip

A few years ago my abbot offered me the opportunity to take a unique journey: a sabbatical year away from my duties as an administrator and teacher of modern languages in our monastery's prep school. So it was that one June morning I packed some clothes, my habit, a breviary, a couple of journals, and a sketchpad, and set off on an eleven-month adventure. Staying mostly in monasteries and religious houses, I trekked from Bavaria to Bolivia, from Amsterdam to Zamora. I climbed snow-clad Swiss Alps, and got soaked by the warm mists of the Iguazu Falls in the Brazilian jungle. I hiked the Highlands above the brooding blackness of Loch Ness and strolled the sweltering banks of the Tiber. I explored the ruins of a castle above the Danube and of a pre-Inca fortress in the Andes. I prayed Vigils in the middle of the night with Cistercian monks on a tiny island in the Mediterranean, and watched the snow sift silently onto the Vienna Opera House.

When I got back to my monastery I discovered that, like a medieval pilgrim returning from Jerusalem or Compostela, I had been deeply affected by my experience. As exciting as my travels had been, the truly important journey had been the inner one of growth and self-discovery: my trip had changed me forever. I began to notice, too, that very often a certain step on that inner journey was connected in my memory with the particular place I'd been visiting at the time I had experienced it. Forty of those special places provide the various settings for the following meditations.

The Spiritual Travelogue

This book weaves the threads of four journeys into a single spiritual travelogue: Lent's journey from Ash Wednesday to Easter serves as the spiritual framework, my sabbatical trip provides a geographical locale for each meditation, the medieval pilgrimage provides the unifying theme, and the journey into my inner self with Christ gives the whole enterprise its ultimate meaning.

Lent and *The Rule of Saint Benedict*

Originally Lent was a period during which the catechumens (candidates for Christian initiation) prepared for their Baptism, which would take place at the Easter Vigil. Before long, however, all Christians began observing Lent as the Church's official season of preparation for Easter. It was a forty-day period characterized by prayer, introspection, almsgiving, self-denial, and the exercise of virtue.

During the middle ages, however, as popular Christian spirituality began to emphasize the sufferings of Christ, the rich variety of Lenten practices was reduced to a single dimension, the penitential: fasting, abstinence from meat, and "giving up" certain things. Although recent scriptural theology and liturgical reforms have helped restore many of the forgotten aspects of Lent, many Christians still see the season almost entirely in terms of the narrower, single-dimensional view.

Benedict of Nursia's *Rule*, written in the sixth century, still provides today's Benedictine women and men with wise guidance for living, and has recently come to be appreciated by Christian lay people as well. The present volume adopts the *Rule's* perspective on Lent, which dates from an era when the observance of Lent was still marked by a rich variety of purposes and practices. Chapter 49, "On the Manner of Keeping Lent," is worth quoting in full:

The life of a monk ought to be a continuous Lent. Since few, however, have the strength for this, we urge the entire community during these days of Lent to keep its manner of life most pure and to wash away in this holy season the negligences of other times. This we can do in a fitting manner by refusing to indulge evil habits and by devoting ourselves to prayer with tears, to reading, to compunction of heart and self-denial. During these days, therefore, we will add to the usual measure of our service something by way of private prayer and abstinence from food or drink, so that each of us will have something above the assigned measure to offer God of his own will with the joy of the Holy Spirit. In other words, let each one deny himself some food, drink, sleep, needless talking and idle jesting, and look forward to holy Easter with joy and spiritual longing.

Everyone should, however make known to the abbot what he intends to do, since it ought to be done with his prayer and approval. Whatever is undertaken without the permission of the spiritual father will be reckoned as presumption and vainglory, not deserving a reward. Therefore, everything must be done with the abbot's approval.

Benedict's treatment reflects the sixth century's notion that Lent is an opportunity to "add to the usual measure of our service," not just by bodily mortification, but by drawing closer to God in prayer, by trying to root out bad habits, and by practicing virtues. In the chapter "On the Daily Manual Labor," he directs that during Lent each monk be given a book to read, and that more time be allotted for reading. Benedict's attitude and approach toward Lent reach back to the days of the catechumens who would "look forward to holy Easter with joy and spiritual longing." It is significant that the only two times the word *gaudium*, "joy," appears in this sober Latin document are in this chapter on Lent, where it refers to the anticipated joy of our goal, "holy Easter."

Besides reflecting the sixth-century theology of Lent, Chapter 49 also reveals some general characteristics of Benedict's *Rule*. First, there is the primacy that he always gives to interior attitude and disposition over mere externals: his Lent is marked more by inner transformation than by outward observances. Second, we see here an instance of his well-known sense of moderation: the abbot is to make sure that the monks do not go to extremes in their Lenten observance. Third, the *Rule* repeatedly challenges the monks to deal honestly and humbly with their own imperfections, and so during Lent they are to "wash away the negligences of other times." Lastly, we should mention Benedict's emphasis on community: Lenten penance in the monastery is a communal exercise, to be celebrated by "the whole community"; no individual may engage in any "private" Lenten practice without the abbot's command.

When Benedict says that "the life of a monk ought to be a continuous Lent," he is offering an insight that is useful for any Christian: whatever we do in Lent (including prayer, holy reading, and acts of charity) is really what we ought to be doing during the rest of the year as well. Thus the meditations in this book are not meant to be confined to Lent, but are designed to be of use at any time of the year.

Since all four of these journeys, the Lenten one, the inward journey with Jesus, the medieval pilgrimage and my sabbatical trip, are more spiritual than geographical, the chapters do not follow a geographical pattern. Rather, the book is organized around six aspects of the wilderness journey of the Israelites, one for each full week in Lent. They are: week one, self-discovery; week two, fighting temptation; week three, the call to conversion; week four, meeting God; week five, depending on the Lord for everything; and week six, arriving in the Promised Land.

It is the author's prayer that the journeys contained in this book will prove a source of joy and blessing for all who choose to join me on the pilgrim road.

THE WEEKDAYS AFTER
ASH WEDNESDAY

Setting Out

Imagine that we are in a church in Le Puy, up in the rugged central mountains of medieval France. The group has been gathering for an hour already and there is a growing feeling of festivity and excitement in the air; we are about to set off on a pilgrimage to the great shrine of Saint James, Santiago de Compostela, in northwest Spain. Many of the people in the church are carrying the walking stick and drinking gourd that mark them as pilgrims; some are wearing a scallop shell, the traditional badge of pilgrims on the difficult and dangerous 800-mile journey over mountains and across desolate uplands to Compostela. There is a spirit of joyful anticipation as we greet friends and check our supplies while waiting for the priest to send us on our way with some words of spiritual advice and encouragement, and, of course, a blessing.

Ash Wednesday and the three days following it were added to the six weeks of Lent in order to reach the symbolic number of forty days of fast and penitence (Sundays were not counted because Christians never fast on Sunday). These four days added on before the first Sunday of Lent now make a sort of "porch," a place for us modern Lenten pilgrims to gather and prepare ourselves for the journey to Easter.

The meditations for these first four days start us on our way with some wise advice for the road. The first meditation, "Canterbury," set in the famous pilgrimage city, sends us off with some encouraging words about staying the course and not turning back once we've begun. "The Channel Tunnel" reminds us that Lent is not a project to be accomplished but rather an opportunity to let God act in us. Next, "La Paz" introduces the important Lenten practice of introspection that we will explore further during the entire first week of Lent. Finally, "Rue de Sèvres" challenges us to make our repentance real by helping others through almsgiving and other works of charity.

The priest calls for quiet. We all fall silent and bow our heads as he extends his hands over our little group and reads from a beautiful old missal this blessing written about the year 1200:

The almighty and everlasting God, who is the Way, the Truth, and the Life, dispose your journey according to his good pleasure; send his angel Raphael to keep you in this your pilgrimage, and both conduct you in peace on your way to the place where you would be, and bring your back again on your return to us in safety.[1]

In a loud voice he chants in Latin, "*Procedamus in pace!*" "Let us proceed in peace."

"*In nomine Domini. Amen!*" we all sing in response, "In the name of the Lord. Amen!"

We all turn and walk silently toward the church door. We are on our way.

---

1. Sarah Hopper, *To Be a Pilgrim: The Medieval Pilgrimage Experience* (Gloucestershire, UK: Sutton Publishing LTD, 2002), 80.

Ash Wednesday

Canterbury, England:
Patrons for the Journey

Canterbury is lively and welcoming this November afternoon. Her streets, lined with pubs and souvenir shops, are noisy with the tongues of a dozen different lands. People still flock to visit the magnificent Gothic cathedral and its tomb of Thomas Becket, just as they've been doing since the late 1100s. Along these bustling lanes once walked the Wife of Bath, the bawdy Miller, the courtly Knight, the Pardoner, and the other colorful pilgrims in Geoffrey Chaucer's *Canterbury Tales*, who told each other stories to pass the time on the road.

But if Canterbury breathes welcome and warmth, she also has an air of Saxon solidity, thanks to her cobblestone pavements, granite fences, moss-covered church walls, and grumpy gray ramparts of rough flint. Canterbury is a stony place.

I've left behind me her bustling streets and crowded pubs. Behind me, too, are the towers of the cathedral and the ancient city walls. I'm off in search of a special spot that hides about a half-mile outside of town.

I turn left up a narrow road that climbs a wooded slope. After a few minutes, a tiny church peeks out from behind the trees on the hilltop. This is

Saint Martin's, the earliest place of continuous Christian worship in all of England. It was already ancient when Bede the Venerable wrote in the early 700s that it was "built of old while the Romans were still inhabiting Britain."

In the year 580, when Canterbury was the capital of the kingdom of Kent, the pagan King Ethelbert married a Christian princess named Bertha. The Queen had an oratory on this spot, and it was here that Ethelbert, now converted to Christianity, was baptized in 598 by Saint Augustine of Canterbury.

Near the crest of the hill I turn up a footpath that leads through the little churchyard and stand for a while looking at the old building. Despite improvements made in the twelfth century, some of the outside walls still show original Roman brickwork.

I walk slowly into the dark, silent chapel, overwhelmed by the sense of holiness of this sacred place whose roots have tapped deep into the rocky Kentish soil since the time of the Romans. All alone in the silence, I sit on a wooden bench and let my imagination wander easily back over the centuries.

Pope Saint Gregory the Great has chosen Augustine, prior of a monastery in Rome, to lead a band of monks to evangelize the pagan territory of the Angles. Their vow of obedience and their missionary zeal speed the little band on their way, full of joy and enthusiasm. But as they travel overland through Gaul, they begin to hear disturbing tales of the savage and murderous English natives. There are graphic details of the strange customs and the unpronounceable tongue that await them. There are sailors' hair-raising reports of the treacherous currents and killer storms that lie in wait for travelers crossing the English Channel. The list of hazards gets longer every day. The missionaries' enthusiasm for their task evaporates like the morning mist, and finally they hold a meeting to discuss whether this mission is really such a good idea after all. Caution wins out: they send Augustine back to Rome to explain to Pope Gregory the impossibility of the task and ask papal permission to return to their monastery in Rome. If Augustine and his little band get their way, the Saxons may have to remain in their pagan darkness for a few more centuries.

But Pope Gregory, the first biographer of Saint Benedict, knows the *Rule for Monks* and its Chapter 68, "The Assignment of Impossible Tasks to a Brother." According to that chapter, if a monk is assigned "a burdensome task, or something he cannot do," he should try it anyway. Then, if it proves beyond his ability, he is to explain humbly to his abbot why he cannot perform the task. Benedict continues: "If after the explanation the superior is still determined to hold to his original order, then the junior must recognize that this is best for him. Trusting in God's help, he must in love obey." We don't know the pope's exact words to Augustine, but we do know that he sends him right back to his companions with a letter of encouragement—and strict orders not to turn around again!

So the monks obediently continue their journey to Britain and today are venerated as the courageous missionary monks who first evangelized England. But it's nice to know that they, too, were subject to an occasional case of cold feet! Like me, they were susceptible at times to discouragement and doubt. Their lives, like mine, included fear as well as faith, defeats as well as victories, weaknesses as well as virtues. The Canterbury monks are the patron saints of people who get cold feet. In the dark vaults of Saint Martin's church, they whisper to me this afternoon to keep up my courage every day and struggle faithfully with my fears and doubts and hesitations.

I bid good-bye to the voices in the chapel and step outside into the chilly churchyard cemetery on the hilltop. Gray clouds still hang low over the roofs and towers of Canterbury below. The first raindrops begin to tap me gently on the shoulder, and I shiver in the November dampness; I turn to head back down to the bus station.

Reflection

Begin this Lenten journey the way Augustine and his monks began their voyage to England, with hope, enthusiasm, and joy. The journey with Jesus into the truth about yourself may not turn out to be as daunting as their trip across the English Channel, but it will certainly have its difficulties.

Think for a few moments about a couple of obstacles you have encountered along the way in past Lents, and ask yourself how you might prepare yourself to overcome them this time. Then compose your own pilgrim's prayer, asking the Lord to bless you as you set out on your journey and bring you to a joyful celebration on Easter morning.

Sacred Scripture (Joel 2:12–13)

"Yet even now, says the LORD, return to me with all your heart, with fasting, with weeping, and with mourning; and rend your hearts and not your clothing. Return to the Lord, your God, for he is gracious and merciful, slow to anger, and abounding in steadfast love, and relents from punishing."

Rule of Benedict (Prologue, vv. 48–49)

"Do not be daunted immediately by fear and run away from the road that leads to salvation. It is bound to be narrow at the outset. But as we progress in this way of life and in faith, we shall run on the path of God's commandments, our hearts overflowing with the inexpressible delight of love."

Thursday after Ash Wednesday

The Channel Tunnel, England: Waiting for the Lord

8:09 a.m. *Ping-pong-ping!* The electronic chimes sound their warning. The shiny silver doors of the Eurostar train slide closed, and we roll smoothly out of Paris' Gare du Nord. On its second day of regular operation, the train smells of new carpeting and upholstery. Everything around me is sparkling and high-tech. This streamlined train, specially designed to run through the new tunnel under the English Channel, will whisk me to Waterloo Station, London, in three hours and six minutes. The sooty slate-blue of the November morning glides past my window as the train hums through suburban Paris.

8:20 a.m. We're now in high gear—186 miles an hour. The farm fields are pouring past like a river of pea soup.

9:36 a.m. An announcement in French and English warns us that in one minute we will be entering the Channel Tunnel. The automatic doors at each end of the car slide closed, and I begin watching for the tunnel entrance. A concrete wall starts running along on our left side, getting higher and higher. I glimpse a part of an arch that covers the tracks like the corner of a giant's mouth. Whoom! We dive into the dark. I look out the big window and see nothing but my own neon-colored reflection in the glass. By shading my eyes against the light and leaning my head against the cold windowpane I can make out a dark brown-gray blur of wall. There won't be anything to see out there for twenty minutes.

9:57 a.m. Sunshine. Welcome to Great Britain. Please turn your watches back one hour. The constant high-pitched whistling sound that the train has been making in the tunnel disappears and the scenery takes up where it left off: rolling hills of green. Sheep graze under a clear blue sky. A strip of black road cuts under the railway, with two cars driving on the wrong side of the road.

9:28 a.m. (British time). Passing through Tonbridge, the first town since Paris to show me its name on a station platform. We are not moving as fast as we were in France, riding on old tracks laid through one of the most densely populated parts of the United Kingdom. In the Channel Tunnel train system, the British tracks are one of the problems still to be solved.

9:44 a.m. We slow to a crawl of maybe sixty miles an hour and glide through Orpington, a town of brick houses and clotheslines that back up onto the tracks. We're still thirty minutes from Waterloo Station.

9:50 a.m. We've stopped. From high up on our embankment we look down onto row houses and a gasworks.

9:51 a.m. The train starts rolling, but very gently now, like a science-fiction monster picking its way carefully among the backyards. Sunshine is bathing the forty-four empty seats—there are only twelve passengers in the car on this almost-maiden voyage.

10:00 a.m. We stop for the second time. It seems odd to be sitting on top of a railway embankment in this sleek futuristic cabin looking down into the narrow wintry backyards of brick row houses. An old man in a gray tweed cap is spading up his garden patch not a hundred feet away. Rich, brown soil, probably nourished with kitchen scraps and lawn clippings.

I'm struck by the contrast between the leisurely pace of his garden and the headlong rush of my high-speed train. The old gardener patiently turns under last summer's stubble to prepare the soil for the winter. Then he'll wait for spring planting time and then wait for the seeds to sprout. Then he'll gently nurture and weed and water his vegetables—and patiently wait for them to ripen.

This train, on the other hand, is designed to cover the greatest distance in the least possible time, delivering passengers efficiently and without ceremony from one city to another. In the process it reduces trees and flowers near the tracks to a nervous blur. For it to actually stop dead on the tracks like this is simply an unthinkable outrage.

It occurs to me that when I set to work at something, I'm a lot like this streamlined train: efficient and effective, zipping along my gleaming rails as fast as I can go. Heaven help anyone or anything that gets in the way.

The man in the tweed cap stops his digging a moment and rests his crossed forearms on top of the spade handle. He squints up toward the shiny metal cars and stares at the twenty-first century, which has just expired up here on the tracks. He is looking right at me. His glance cuts through the window and touches me like an icy finger. A moment later, he turns back to his gardening.

If my life is like this speedy Eurostar, then being on this sabbatical year is sort of like being stalled on the tracks. I'm able to pause and look at myself. This morning this old gentleman and his little garden are challenging me to examine my approach to life. He moves slowly, while I rush around at 186 miles an hour. He spends most of his time waiting patiently—for spring to arrive, for seeds to sprout, for tomatoes to ripen. I spend all my energy trying to make things happen on or ahead of schedule and according to my specifications. He works gently within the limits of the situation—a tiny patch of land, a given kind of soil, a certain amount of sunshine, his own decreasing strength. I fight my limits on every side—squeezing more minutes into one hour, reaching beyond the bounds of my own physical and mental energy, refusing to accept that certain things are just the way they are. . . .

10:08 a.m. The Eurostar begins laboring forward at walking speed. We tiptoe through the tiny suburban station of Kent House, with tarmac platforms closing in on both sides.

10:14 a.m. We're now late. *Ping-pong-ping!* "Ladies and gentlemen, due to certain difficulties, we will be traveling at a slower speed than usual. We are sorry for any inconvenience this may cause."

10:17 a.m. We leave the residential suburban scene and jump into a dark tunnel where we pick up some speed. I wonder what the engineer's thinking right now as he gazes at his flickering computer screen. The Eurostar travels so fast that visual train signals along the track become useless blurs; the engineer has to rely on a computer screen for all his information.

I have to admit that sometimes I start zipping along so fast that I can't see any of the warning lights, and I miss important signals about slowing down for my own good or for the sake of others around me.

10:20 a.m. Out of the short tunnel . . . Sydenham Hill station . . . Herne Hill . . . apartment buildings and row houses . . . worn-out neighborhoods of brick and asphalt . . . rough, shuddering tracks . . . A double-decker bus below . . . a wide river alongside—probably the Thames.

I think about the little man in the gray cap, and a snatch of Scripture from the prophet Jeremiah comes to mind. God's chosen ones, he declares, "will be like a well-watered garden." Hmm. . . . What if I were less like a speeding train and more like a watered garden?

If my life were a garden, then my heart would be a place of calm, patient waiting for things to come in their own due time: seasons of blossoms, seasons of plenty, and seasons of sleet and snow and seeming sterility. If my life were a garden to be tended, then my desire to control everything would no longer make sense, because a garden can't be forced or pushed or hurried along; a garden needs to be nurtured, not driven headlong like a train on a track. Then my efforts at prayer or work would take on a different meaning, because anything that a garden produces comes not as my accomplishment but as a mysterious, beautiful gift of nature's bounty.

I'm startled by the familiar electronic bell: *Ping-pong-ping!*

The triumphant announcement comes in two languages—we're arriving at Waterloo Station, London. . . . sorry for any problems caused by the delay. My ticket says, "Arrival Waterloo Int 10:13." We're pulling in at 10:35.

Being twenty-two minutes late is really embarrassing if you're an express train, but it's not so important if you're a well-watered garden.

Reflection

If your life is a garden, then Lent is not a project to be accomplished, but rather an opportunity to let God help you to look carefully at your garden and help it be more fruitful. Prayer, fasting, and works of charity are traditional ways of doing this. If your life is a garden that needs to be watered and weeded but cannot be forced or controlled, ask the Lord to help you this Lent to let go of your need to control, and to teach you how to be patient with the God's slow way of doing things.

Is there an area of your life where you tend to be especially impatient? Think of the people you interact with most often. This Lent try to treat each of them like a well-watered garden in need of nurturing.

Sacred Scripture (Isa. 58:11, NAB)

"Then the Lord will guide you always and give you plenty even on the parched land. He will renew your strength, and you shall be like a watered garden, like a spring whose water never fails."

Rule of Benedict (Prologue, v. 4)

"First of all, every time you begin a good work, you must pray to God most earnestly to bring it to perfection."

Friday after
Ash Wednesday

La Paz Witches' Market, Bolivia:
Trusting in God Alone

La Paz, Bolivia, sits in a bowl-shaped valley 12,000 feet up in the Andes. Hundreds of tiny brick houses climb the steep slopes like a tattered blanket of brown ivy.

Iris, our private guide, is escorting three of us on an afternoon tour of La Paz, the world's highest capital. With me are a young Chilean couple, Carlos and Elena. We've left our hired taxi for a few minutes to stroll up a cobblestone street in an old quarter of town. Its official name is Calle Linares, but everyone calls it "*el Mercado de las Brujas*," "the Witches' Market." The street is lined with little shops and sidewalk stalls displaying love potions, magic charms, animal skins, medicines, and folk remedies. Iris explains that all of these have been used for centuries in *Aymara*, the native Andean culture.

Women in bright-colored ankle-length skirts and tiny bowler hats stand watch over their wares as potential customers and foreign tourists file past.

"What are those?" asks Elena, as she holds tightly onto Carlos's arm and points at some odd-looking dried up objects in a cardboard box.

"Those are dried frogs," answers Iris. "They're supposed to be good for attracting money."

Looking up the street at the unbroken row of stalls and shops, I ask her, "So, all the people running these shops are witches?"

"Not necessarily. Some are medicine women; others are folk doctors, or astrologers. There are fortunetellers, too, and sorcerers."

Suddenly she stands still and tilts her head back slightly. "Can you smell the smoke?" she asks. "That's from the animal sacrifices."

I sniff the thin mountain air but can't smell anything in particular. I'm glad, though, that she's stopped walking for a few moments: I'm short of breath, and I'm getting a little light-headed. These are typical symptoms of *soroche*, altitude sickness. Having been here only twenty-four hours, I'm still getting used to being two miles up. I've been noticing the strange quality of the sunlight up here, too: it's clear, almost harsh, but in a watery sort of way that's hard to describe.

"What was that old lady back there saying to us?" asks Carlos, who doesn't seem bothered by the altitude.

"She was inviting you to come into her shop and offer a sacrifice to Pachamama, Mother Earth, to ask for health and happiness." Carlos gives a noncommittal grunt and walks on.

We wander over to a sidewalk display that is being tended by an old woman with a wide, toothless smile. She boasts about the powers of her toad talismans, owl feathers, and stone amulets. Then comes the sales pitch for the different colored candles, which release their magical powers when lighted: the blue candle brings good luck at work, the yellow promises health, the green one money, and the purple one happiness. When she invites us to step into her tiny store, we decline politely and turn to move on. I get a quick peek, though, through the open door into the shadowy interior; a dusty stuffed armadillo rests on a shelf beside a random collection of dozens of old liquor bottles containing murky, odd-colored liquids.

We move farther up the street, walking behind a young Bolivian woman. Like many of her sisters, she is using a cloth draped over her shoulders to carry a large bundle on her back. The bright red blanket with yellow and blue stripes glows in the afternoon sun, bouncing gently as she walks. Just as I start to wonder what she might be carrying in there, a baby's head pops out; from under a thatch of coarse black hair, two big brown eyes blink curiously at me. I can't help laughing with delight at such a charming little surprise. A moment later the tiny head disappears again under the blanket.

Off to my left I notice two strange, shriveled objects hanging on the outside wall of a shop. I've already seen several of these in the stalls along the street. Brittle, dark brown carcasses almost two feet long, they remind me vaguely of the skinned rabbits I'd seen hanging in the windows of French butcher shops. I ask, "Iris, what are those things?"

"¡Ah, Si! Those are dried llama fetuses," she explains. Shocked but fascinated, I take a closer look; I can make out the bulging eyeballs. Our guide continues, "They have a lot of uses. Many Bolivians wouldn't think of building a new house without burying a llama fetus in the foundation."

Suddenly I start to feel uneasy—I begin to see the quaint, colorful scene in a different light: all these talismans and candles and spells are human attempts to control the spiritual powers that affect our lives.

Witches claim to understand how these mysterious forces work, and claim to be able, for a small fee, to direct and control them for us.

Christians try to leave themselves as vulnerable as possible to God. Some of the things we do in the monastery, in fact, are meant precisely to help us put our lives in the Lord's hands. For example, the common ownership of goods and our frugal lifestyle remind us to rely on God rather than on possessions or pleasures. When a new monk professes his vows, he stands at the altar in front of the rest of the community and with hands stretched toward heaven sings three times, "Sustain me, O Lord, as you have promised, that I may live. Disappoint me not in my hope!" Far from trying to manipulate God, the new monk is crying out publicly, asking the Loving One to guard him and support him all his days—especially on days when events are beyond his own control or understanding.

In the *mercado de las brujas*, on the other hand, you try to do exactly the opposite: you hope to gain the upper hand over the great mysterious powers of the universe and make them subject to *you*. There is nothing here that gives your life a deeper meaning, nothing that challenges you to become more fully human, nothing that calls you to self-sacrificing generosity toward your neighbor.

"*¡Aqui estámos!* Here we are!" Iris announces. We've come to the other end of the street, where our taxi is waiting for us. As we climb in, Iris tells the driver, "*Vamos pues a la iglesia de San Francisco*—let's go to the church of Saint Francis." "Good," I think to myself, "a visit with the humble patron saint of animals will be a pleasant contrast to the witches' market with its llama fetuses and dead armadillos."

The old Ford taxi lurches ferociously into the traffic, its horn blaring. We barely miss an old woman bent under a giant bundle of weird black leaves. When she turns her head slowly and skewers our driver with an ominous stare, it crosses my mind that if we had hit her, it would probably have meant months of very bad luck for all of us.

Reflection

Lent is a good time to stroll into your own personal witches' market. Walk in and take a careful inventory of the things you tend to rely on when God is not enough, or when God is not answering as quickly as you would like. Make a list of two or three, and sit with it for awhile. Are there things or behaviors on your list which you could easily get rid of by simply "fasting from" them during Lent? If there is one that has been there for a long time, ask the Lord to help you to let go of it.

Ask God to help you to stop relying on created things and depend on the Lord alone. You might try standing up and extending your hands toward heaven and praying three times, "Sustain me, O Lord, as you have promised that I may live. Disappoint me not in my hope!"

Sacred Scripture (Deut. 30:17–20, RSV)

But if your heart turns away, and you will not hear, but are drawn away to worship other gods and serve them, I declare to you this day, that you shall perish; you shall not live long in the land which you are going over the Jordan to enter and possess. I call heaven and earth to witness against you this day, that I have set before you life and death, blessing and curse; therefore choose life, that you and your descendants may live, loving the LORD your God, obeying his voice, and cleaving to him; for that means life to you and length of days.

Rule of Benedict
(Chapter 4, "The Tools for Good Works," v. 4)

"Place your hope in God alone."

Saturday after
Ash Wednesday

Rue de Sèvres, Paris:
Putting Faith into Action

Number 95, rue de Sèvres, is a charming rabbit warren of buildings. Since 1817 it has been the mother house of Les Pères de la Mission (the Vincentians), founded in 1625 by Saint Vincent de Paul. The Order has since spread around the world, bringing the Good News to the poor. Vincentians of all ages come and go in the hallways, speaking French, Spanish, English, or any of a number of other languages. Many are here for ongoing refresher courses in the theology of their order.

Paris

Vincent was born in 1581 into a peasant family in a village of south-western France. As a young priest, he arrived in Paris and became chaplain to the rich and influential Gondi family. Then one day he was called to the bedside of a dying peasant. There he came face-to-face with the horrid reality of the squalor and misery of the French peasants. He began to organize help for the poor and the sick, and to preach the message of God's love to the simple folk on the Gondi estates. From this point, his life would never be the same.

The mother house's unremarkable gray façade hides some pleasant secrets from the passing pedestrian. Many of the rooms have recently been renovated, and the spacious garden area offers the opportunity for a quiet stroll among flowers and trees. At one end of the building is the sober church built in 1827. Above the high altar is a beautiful silver casket containing the remains of the saint, transferred from Notre Dame de Paris in 1830.

Vincent enlisted the help of pious women in his struggle against the poverty and suffering of the peasants, and his work soon expanded beyond the Gondi estate to reach the poor in the entire countryside and then eventually in the cities as well. In 1633, with Louise de Marillac, Vincent founded the Daughters of Charity. He and Louise composed a Rule and gave conferences as the sisters became more and more invaluable collaborators with him in helping orphans, the sick, and the hungry.

In a hallway not far from the reception desk hangs a large map of the city of Paris. Small red dots are sprinkled evenly over its entire surface. Reading the legend at the bottom I see that each dot marks a place in Paris that was somehow touched by Saint Vincent during his life: an orphanage founded, starving people fed, a hospital staffed with sisters, a retreat preached, a school begun. There are dozens of these dots, each one telling a story of charity, of boundless energy, of commitment to spreading God's love on earth.

Vincent de Paul was not a profound thinker; he had no great original insights. Yet few people have ever accomplished as much with their lives. His success was due to his great natural abilities, of course, and to a staggering capacity for work. But as I stare at the old map, I begin to understand the secret of Vincent's success: these dots are actually the fallout of Vincent's spiritual life. I can hear him insisting in one of his conferences, "You must start by establishing the kingdom of God in yourself first, and only then in other people." I hear him echoing Saint Benedict's emphasis on the importance of the interior life over externals when he says to the members of his religious communities, "You have to aim at the interior life, and if you're missing that, you're missing everything." Vincent, like Benedict, was always aware of God's constant presence when trying to help the poor, when agonizing over a difficult decision, or when suffering from the slanderous accusations of jealous enemies.

His intense prayer life had a surprising result: instead of becoming a visionary lost in the clouds of contemplation, he became a man of deeds.

Vincent believed in the "indispensable priority of action." He didn't move from principles to practice or from insight to deeds; he simply began with love. This is the key to understanding his tremendous ability to get things done.

I find myself full of religious thoughts, pious ideas, and abstract principles that need to be applied. But of course much of this spiritual theorizing never finds its way into practice, and never changes my way of living. Vincent's formula was simple: Start with love. Love is both a guiding principle and an action.

Vincent's great works for the poor were not his reason for existing— God was. He didn't go around giving his life to the poor—he gave it to God. Because Vincent de Paul knew he was loved by God, he could love God in return, and could cover this map of Paris with all these lovely dots.

The gospel calls us to a life of love. Each of us, whatever our state in life, is expected to leave a bunch of red dots sprinkled across the map of our own life, marking places where our love has made a difference, made God's love real for others. I start to wonder what my own map looks like.

I hear a door open at the other end of the long corridor and see my Vincentian friend coming down the hall to greet me. I turn away from the map with a quick prayer to Saint Vincent that I might, like him, leave a little bit of divine fallout on the map when I die.

Reflection

Lent is traditionally a time for growing closer to God through acts of charity toward others, especially those in need. How do you live out Vincent's simple formula, "Start with love," in your life?

Imagine a map of the region where you are living, or where you lived for a long time. Would there be a lot of red dots on it marking places where you were Christ for others through your kind deeds, gentle words, and loving actions? Would there be a section where there are few red dots, or even none?

The traditional practices of fasting and almsgiving always go together. Think of someone or some group of people who could benefit from your charity during this Lent; make a Lenten resolution to be of help to them.

Sacred Scripture (Isa. 58:5–8, NAB)

Is this the manner of fasting I wish, of keeping a day of penance: That a man bow his head like a reed, and lie in sackcloth and ashes? Do you call this a fast, a day acceptable to the LORD? This, rather, is the fasting that I wish: releasing those bound unjustly, untying the thongs of the yoke; Setting free the oppressed, breaking every yoke; Sharing your bread with the hungry, sheltering the oppressed and the homeless; Clothing the naked when you see them, and not turning your back on your own.

Wisdom of the Desert

A monk once posed this question to an elder: "There are two brothers, one of whom remains praying in his cell, fasting six days at a time and doing a great deal of penance. The other one takes care of the sick. Which one's work is more pleasing to God?" The elder replied: "If that brother who fasts six days at a time were to hang himself up by the nose, he could not equal the one who takes care of the sick."[2]

---

2. Thomas Merton, trans., *The Wisdom of the Desert: Sayings from the Desert Fathers of the Fourth Century* (New York: New Direction Books, 1970), 132.

THE FIRST WEEK OF LENT

Meeting My True Self

The Israelites' journey through the wilderness stripped away all of their illusions, so that they could see who they truly were. It brought them face-to-face with the stark reality of their weakness, their unfaithfulness, and their forgetfulness.

Many pilgrims made the long journey to Jerusalem, Rome, or Compostela as a means to atone for their sins. As early as the 800s, when traveling was an uncomfortable and dangerous business, pilgrimages were often imposed as penances, even by civil authorities, for certain sins or crimes.

Like the Israelites in the desert or those penitent pilgrims, we must begin our own inner journey of conversion with the honest acknowledgement that we, too, are flawed and sinful creatures in need of God's healing and redemption. The meditations for this first week of Lent help us to face and deal with the fact that we are indeed broken and imperfect. "Muros," "Dieppe," and "Fátima" all help us to see the central role that our imperfections play in our spiritual life. "Alba de Tormes" reflects on the value of healthy, heartfelt humility; and "Berlin" challenges us to look into our hearts to find and break down any barriers to love. Finally, "Saint Julien" urges us to let go of our need to be perfect.

Monday of the
First Week of Lent

Muros, Spain:
Using Low Tide

The afternoon bus from La Coruña is weaving its way south down the ragged coast of northwestern Spain. The scenery is a kaleidoscope of mountain slopes, evergreen groves, and stony seacoast.

Straight ahead spreads a broad dark-blue bay, and beyond it soar high brown mountains, clad to the waist in dark pine forests. Each isolated house along the narrow road salutes us with a line of bright-colored laundry that flutters sideways in the strong sea wind. Shrunken old ladies in black sit in a row, their backs against the wall of the village church, catching the late afternoon sun. Here and there a stranded palm tree stands beside the road as if waiting for a ride from a friend. On a headland to our right, a lighthouse pops out of a lush green meadow. Just off shore, a black fishing boat beetles across the dark green sea. A wide, silver beach peeks playfully from behind the tall straight trunks of a pine grove.

As we round a bend, the next panorama opens up in the distance: lofty gray mountains dotted with greenery encircle a wide cove. White two-story buildings with red tile roofs are strung in a necklace that lies along the road, hugging the horseshoe of the harbor. Their windows face the street and look across it to the waterfront and the bay. Above the row of red roofs, other houses climb the steep granite slope.

Halfway around the horseshoe, the bus drops me off and continues on its way toward Orense. I stand still for a moment to enjoy the smell of the cool sea air. Seagulls skim and soar, scolding the bright-colored fishing boats that are resting at their docks. The quiet, black water sloshes lazily against the rocks lining the shore. This is Muros. I've come here to visit the grandmother of two of my students. I introduced myself to her by phone from Santiago de Compostela two days ago, and have now shown up to impose on her hospitality.

A friendly passerby points me in the right direction. As it turns out, though, the street name I give her actually refers to a whole maze of lanes and pathways that crisscross the hillside farther along the curve of the bay. To add to my confusion, house numbers seem to be assigned somewhat haphazardly, and I need the help of a second neighbor woman to locate my destination, which turns out to be high up on the steep slope.

At last I find myself saying hello to the grandmother: "*¡Buenas tardes, Abuela!*" Her daughter, who is visiting from America, soon stops by to say hello and chat. Grandma's generous supper, combined with the salt air and the fatigue of the long bus ride, makes me ready for bed soon after we leave the table. My room is upstairs, at the front of the house. Its window faces the bay, though there's nothing but inky darkness outside when I turn off the light.

The harsh cries of the seagulls wake me. A dull, silver dawn is just starting to filter through the little window. Impatient for my first look at the harbor from up here on the hillside I climb out of bed, put on my glasses, and shuffle sleepily across the room, noticing the tangy smell of the sea. As I gently brush aside the white curtains I blink in disbelief. The bay is gone!

At the bottom of the slope stretches more than half a mile of ugly mud and wet sand. Far out from the shore a tractor and a dump truck slide noiselessly over the brown muck that was water last night. Several men are working busily with rakes and shovels near the truck.

After breakfast I thank *la Abuela* and say good-bye for the day. Gray rain clouds are gathering on the horizon as I start down the twisting lanes to inspect the disaster scene at the waterfront. I reach the bottom of the hillside, cross the road, and sit down at the edge of the mud on a bench that last evening looked out over silky ripples. And I start to reflect.

For me the "real" Muros is the picturesque one I saw yesterday: the beautiful bay full of sparkling waves lapping at the rocks along the beach front. The bleak sight before me now is some sort of blunder: it's supposed to be a glistening expanse of saltwater, not an unsightly wasteland of dark-brown muck strewn with small boats lying on their sides like dead birds. This isn't the way a fishing port is supposed to look.

The more I get used to the scene, however, the more I start to realize that there is nothing wrong with it at all: this is exactly what Muros is supposed to look like—when the tide is out!

My life, it occurs to me, is not so different. It, too, has its high and low tides. I usually see the good times, when life is a joy and the tide is full, as the way life is "supposed to be." The other times, when the tide is out, are simply unwanted interruptions. I resent the periods of mud and suffering; I try to just ignore them until the tide rolls back in.

In a coastal town, though, high tide and low tide are two equally important realities. It's not that one or the other is the way the sea is supposed to be; each one offers its own opportunities. Low tide is the time for clam diggers to go out to find clams, and for mussel farmers to harvest their shellfish from the wooden posts that stand in the sea bed near shore. In the case of Muros, low tide means something else as well: the workers with their tractor and truck, I was told at breakfast, are removing the residue of an oil spill that fouled the coast years before. They take advantage of low tide every day to drive out to the polluted part of the bay floor and clean it up some more. Then, as the tide comes flooding back in, they beat a retreat and wait for the next low water.

Heavy clouds are now looming closer every minute—Galicia is famous for its rainy climate. When they hear the word *Gallego* (a Galician), most Spaniards automatically picture someone carrying a furled umbrella, ready for the next shower.

Perhaps, I think, as I look out at the acres of mud flats stretching in front of me, we actually learn more about ourselves when the tide of our life is low than when it is high—because a lot more of the bay is exposed to view. This is why Benedict insists that we admit our mistakes: because they help us recognize the important and undeniable fact that we're imperfect.

Times of sadness, strain, disappointment, and tragedy let us see certain truths about ourselves that we'd never have noticed otherwise; things about us that need changing stand out especially starkly in the brown mud. Low tide isn't particularly pleasant or pretty, but it is wonderfully revealing. It would be a shame to waste this precious time just hanging around waiting for the next high tide.

My supervision of the workmen comes to a sudden halt when a large gray cloud starts to dump the first shower of the day. I quickly unfold my little black umbrella and scurry toward a nearby coffee shop, leaving the low-tide laborers to their cleanup.

Reflection

In the hunger, thirst, and wandering of the wilderness years, the Israelites learned who God was for them. Think of some "low tide" experience such as a serious illness or the loss of a job. What did it teach you about yourself and your relationship with God?

Just as the receding tide leaves the bed of the bay exposed to view, the fasting, prayer, reading, and other disciplines of Lent can help expose parts of your inner self that you might not ordinarily get to see—and it's not always pretty. Ask the Lord to help you to look at some things about yourself that may need attention.

Sacred Scripture (John 8:32)

"You will know the truth, and the truth will make you free."

Rule of Benedict
(Chapter 4, "The Tools for Good Works," vv. 42–43)

"If you notice something good in yourself, give credit to God, not to yourself, but be certain that the evil you commit is always your own and yours to acknowledge."

Tuesday of the
First Week of Lent

Dieppe, France:
Being Unfinished

The sturdy brick houses of this newer section of Dieppe, up in the hills east of the old town, are designed to keep out the damp and chill that are so typical of Normandy. As we drive to church this Sunday morning I say to my hosts, "Well, maybe there'll be some sunshine later today." I've been staying with Bernard and Colette for almost a week, and I still haven't seen the sun.

For me, the name Dieppe conjures up black-and-white images of smoldering ruins and beaches littered with charred invasion vehicles. In 1942, a Canadian force attempted a beach landing in German-occupied Normandy a couple of miles west of here. The operation cost a thousand lives, but the Allied commanders got what they'd hoped to get: knowledge about amphibious landings on the shores of Normandy. The lessons learned at Dieppe would pay off two years later during the historic "D-Day" invasion.

We arrive at the neighborhood church, where I am introduced to the pastor and invited to concelebrate the Sunday Eucharist with him. Since we have a few minutes before Mass starts, Bernard proudly shows me around his parish church. There's not a whole lot to see: it's a large brick structure with pleasant rounded arches running down both sides of the central nave. As we're walking toward the sacristy, he points out the pillars that support the arches. "You see how the columns near the altar are perfectly smooth cylinders? Well, now look at the ones toward the back."

When I turn around and look out into the body of the church, I see what he's getting at: the rest of the pillars are different. They're not smooth, cylindrical columns but rather twelve-sided pillars, with a dozen flat facets running top to bottom.

"Some people say that the original plan was for all the columns to be rounded smoothly like the ones up front here, but they ran short of cash.

So to save money they didn't round off the rest of the pillars but left them unfinished, with all those flat sides."

Time to get vested. In a few minutes I'm walking out into the sanctuary to concelebrate Sunday Mass with the parish priest. I spot Bernard and Colette in the congregation. A few rows in front of them is the old gentleman who came by yesterday and described in vivid detail over a glass of port what it was like the day the Canadians landed. Across the aisle from him several African girls from a nearby boarding school stand stiffly in their pew. We all sit down for the readings and the sermon.

I look out toward the crowded pews, and I notice those unfinished pillars—twelve-sided, incomplete. It occurs to me that this is an unfinished church. It will always be unfinished.

Then, as I study the faces in the congregation, I realize that we're all members of an unfinished Church. We, the People of God, will never be quite perfect—at least not this side of heaven. Ours will always be an incomplete Church—always striving toward perfection, and always falling short. Just like this parish church building, the Church on earth will never be finished.

The sermon is over, and we stand and pray a litany of intentions for various needs, the whole congregation responding, "*Seigneur, exauce-nous!*"—"Lord, hear us!" We sit again and sing an offertory hymn as two parishioners bring up the bread and wine to be used on the altar.

The main reason that the Church is unfinished, of course, is that we humans are ourselves perpetually unfinished. We've all experienced the sense that there is always something more to learn, to accomplish, to become. It is this "incurable unfinishedness," as one philosopher calls it, that sets us apart from other living things, because in trying to "finish" ourselves, we become creators. Our incurable unfinishedness keeps us childlike, capable of learning and growing. We may be trying to head toward perfection, but none of us will ever arrive there.

Benedict understands this, and is constantly making allowances for human weakness and frailty. For example, although he would prefer that monks abstain from wine altogether, he admits that "monks of our day cannot be convinced of this" and so he allows for a certain amount of wine to be allotted each day. Similarly, after saying "a monk's life ought to be a continual Lent" he concedes that "few have the virtue for this, so let us at least keep the forty days of Lent in a special way."

I look again at one of the twelve-sided columns, and it occurs to me that not only is imperfection okay, it's our unique strong point. We're supposed to be unfinished! Humans exist in the gap between what is and what could be, between the reality and the dream, the already and the not-yet. And it is precisely in this gap that the saints are made. Virtue presumes that we are not yet at the ideal: virtue is the struggle to close the gap between what we are and what we're called to be—we can be virtuous, we can be saints, only if we're imperfect.

Prayer is our spirit's response to the experience of the gap, of being "hungry for God." The psalmist prays in Ps. 42, "As a deer longs for flowing streams, so my soul longs for you, O God." We can only pray if we are unfinished.

Imperfections, setbacks, and sins, then, are all part of the striving; they're all grist for the mill. They're the place where we are destined to meet God—in the gap. Wherever there is that unfinishedness, there is the call to holiness: in the kitchen, the office, the hospital room, or the supermarket. Wherever there is that sense of striving, there is a saint in the making. From this point of view, then, there is no such thing as an "obstacle" to sainthood. Saints may be preoccupied with raising a family and balancing the checkbook; we may be struggling with our too-crowded daily schedule, our short temper, or our jealousy; we may have to live with a painful experience in the past or a physical disability. No matter what, it is through and in the experience of our imperfections that God wants to meet us.

We stand now for the Eucharistic Prayer, the most solemn part of the Mass. The church is filled with the melody of the angelic hymn, "*Saint! Saint! Saint!*"—"Holy! Holy! Holy!" I look out at the people singing. Here are saints with cares and trials, problems and sins, shortcomings and fears. Here is the Church.

A ray of warm, golden light bursts through a window to my left. The sun at last! It highlights a twelve-sided pillar, one of those unfinished columns in an unfinished church filled with unfinished saints.

Reflection

Fasting and other forms of Lenten "self-denial" let us experience in our bodies our own unfinishedness, our incompleteness. They leave us hungry and wishing for something to fill up what is missing. These practices are not based on body-hating or on despising created reality; rather, they are reminders that we are not yet complete, that we are still on the way toward the fullness of the Kingdom.

Where do you meet your own unfinishedness most clearly in your daily life? Is there a particular fault or flaw of yours that you find disheartening? How might you use Lent to work with God at closing one particular gap between the way you are and the way God intended you to be?

Sacred Scripture (Matt. 11:28, RSV)

"Come to me, all who labor and are heavy laden, and I will give you rest."

Rule of Benedict
(Chapter 64, "The Election of an Abbot," v. 13)

"[The abbot] is to distrust his own frailty and remember not to crush the bruised reed."

Wednesday of the First Week of Lent

Fátima, Portugal:
Dealing with the Real

The train south from Coimbra, Portugal, to Fátima is a real "local," calling at every little village. We arrive fifty-five minutes late at the station marked "Fátima." That's when I find out that the railroad station is called "Fátima" not because it's located in or anywhere near the town of that name, but because it's as close as you can get by train. I soon learn that I still have another twenty-some miles to go, and that the only practical way is by taxi for the flat rate of $20 one-way.

coimbra - Portugal

The ride along winding roads through the rugged mountain country of central Portugal finally brings me to the real Fátima; as he drops me off, the friendly taxi driver points me toward a wide sidewalk that cuts between two large buildings. Two minutes later I'm standing in a vast plaza that is awash with warm spring sunlight. Off to my right, the basilica, begun in 1928, extends its huge semicircular porticoes like welcoming arms to embrace Mary's visitors who come to her shrine from all parts of the world. I immediately climb the stairs and walk slowly into the great church. The interior is surprisingly bright, thanks to the light-colored stone of its walls. I walk around for a few minutes, then sit and pray for a few more.

As I step back out into the fresh spring sunshine, a wide expanse of empty pavement spreads downhill before me like a great gray meadow, awaiting the return of the huge throngs of summer pilgrims.

Today, respectful visitors are sprinkled in small handfuls around the plaza, strolling slowly in different directions as they enjoy the first real taste of spring. The atmosphere is serene—there is an unmistakable air of prayerfulness and peace.

I set off down the stairs and across the immense plaza toward a modern concrete-and-glass canopy, open on three sides. I walk in under the roof and sit on one of the wooden pews arranged in a horseshoe around a square area bounded by a wooden railing. Inside this sanctuary stands a short pillar of white marble that supports a statue of Our Lady of Fátima. This is the true hub of Fátima, the focal point for four million visitors a year, because it marks the exact location of the bush on which stood the "lady more brilliant than the sun" that May afternoon in 1917. The little bush has long ago been reverently pulled to pieces by eager hands.

As the miraculous appearances continued through the summer of 1917, more and more people came to wait with little ten-year-old Lucia and her cousins, Francisco and Jacinta. At the final apparition, on October 13, 1917, about 70,000 people were here in the Cova da Iria to see what would happen. The Lady appeared as promised, and told the children that she was "The Lady of the Rosary." She asked that a chapel be built here in her honor. At the end of the apparition, everyone present saw the miracle that Our Lady had promised the children: "the sun, resembling a silver disc, could be gazed at without difficulty and, whirling on itself like a wheel of fire, it seemed about to fall upon the earth."

Well, those first visitors are gone, and of the three children only Lucia, now a Carmelite nun in a convent in Coimbra, is still alive. The meadow of the Cova da Iria has changed beyond recognition. But behind the large canopy where I'm sitting, you can still see the oak tree under which the children used to pray the rosary while waiting for the promised appearances on the thirteenth of each month. The other authentic reminder of the great events of 1917 stands in front of me in the sanctuary, a few feet behind the statue. It is a little country chapel, a tiny oratory that looks as if it might seat about eighteen people. The Lady had commanded that a church be built here in her honor, and this white chapel was the answer to her request.

A constant stream of visitors flows in and out under the canopy. Parents with tiny children in tow come to pray the rosary; a few older people, stooped under the weight of cares and years, just sit in quiet meditation. I've got plenty of company as I pray a rosary for my long list of relatives and friends.

I sit gazing at the whitewashed chapel. It *is* awfully modest. Could this possibly be what Mary had in mind when she asked that a church be built in her honor? They must have misunderstood. She must have meant "build me a magnificent marble basilica glowing with gold and precious stones."

A whole busload of pilgrims from Italy surges in to kneel near the statue in front of the chapel, but the silence remains unbroken. I start to pray the First Joyful Mystery of the rosary, "the Annunciation," meditating on the scene in Luke's gospel in which Mary is asked to become the mother of the Messiah, to carry the Son of God in her womb.

A leaflet on the bench in front of me catches my eye. Along the bottom in large type are Our Lady of Fátima's words in English, "Build me a church!" I begin to think that maybe God asks the same of each of us: "Make yourself into a dwelling place for me." So, I'm supposed to be, like Mary, a holy sanctuary, an abode of the Divine?

Immediately, I start mumbling excuses, trying to get out of the assignment: I have nothing to build with . . . I don't have any heroic virtues or remarkable abilities. In fact, I have a few pretty glaring faults. You can't build a basilica with what I've got to offer—just look at me! All I can bring to the project are things like my short temper, my big ego, and my distractions at prayer. Imperfections and struggles aren't fit materials for building a dwelling place for God.

I look up and gaze more closely at the simple chapel in front of me, the first one built in response to Our Lady's request for a church. You can't really call it a church compared with the great buildings I've seen in my travels. To be perfectly frank, it's actually just one of those humble, rustic oratories you find all over the European countryside.

But then, Mary of Nazareth was a country girl from a small village herself. When she asked the poor farmers around the Cova da Iria to make her a church, she must have known that they couldn't afford anything big or showy, no stained glass or Italian marble. The local people understood her request perfectly and they built her church with what they had at hand—local stone, wood from the forest, and sand from the river. This little oratory is exactly what Our Lady of Fátima had in mind.

In my own struggle to become a sanctuary for God to dwell in, the plain white chapel of Fátima's farmers has a comforting message for me: build your church with what you've got! Don't mourn the fact that you have no marble or silver or stained glass, but give God what you have at hand—your everyday life, with all its limitations and failings. I think of what Benedict, with his down-to-earth wisdom, might say. "Of course you have distractions during prayer, but you just keep praying anyway. Of course you sometimes lose your temper with your kids, but you keep on guiding and loving them anyway. Of course your daily work isn't always done as thoroughly as it should be, but you keep working anyway."

The last bead of my rosary slides between my fingers. The end of the Fifth Joyful Mystery, "the Finding of Jesus in the Temple." I glance at my watch and realize that it's almost time to find a taxi for the return ride to the station. I take a last look at the chapel, then walk out onto the wide sunlit plaza. Up to my left looms the great basilica with its impressive colonnades. I think of Mary's request, "Build me a church!"

I try to picture the church that I'm supposed to be building with my life, given what I've got to work with. It's not exactly a basilica. In fact, it looks a lot like, well, that little white chapel behind me.

Reflection

On our journey with Christ into our deepest self, we discover our shortcomings and faults. These turn out to be the building blocks of our spiritual life. How has God used an imperfection of yours to draw closer to you in love? How has the Lord used your brokenness to help you see your need for God? How has God used your own weakness to help you appreciate how much God cares for you?

Think of some particular imperfection of yours, maybe one that really bothers you; ask God to show you how you are to use that imperfection to build a temple for the Lord.

Sacred Scripture (1 Cor. 3:16–17)

"Do you not know that you are God's temple and that God's Spirit dwells in you?

If any one destroys God's temple, God will destroy that person. For God's temple is holy, and you are that temple."

Wisdom of the Egyptian Desert

A devil changed himself into a bright angel and appeared to a monk. "I am the angel Gabriel," he lied, "and I have been sent to you." But the brother wasn't about to be taken in, and replied, "Think again—you must have been sent to somebody else. I haven't done anything to deserve an angel!" In the face of this realistic self assessment the devil had to retreat.

Thursday of the First Week of Lent

Alba de Tormes: Being Humble

Old Padre Angel believes that no self-respecting Christian should spend a month studying in Salamanca without at some point traveling to the nearby town of Alba de Tormes to visit the tomb of Saint Teresa of Avila. So this afternoon I'm riding in the front seat as he drives me on my mandatory half-hour pilgrimage across the gently rolling farm country of Castile y Leon in north-central Spain.

Alba lies on a gentle slope above the River Tormes. A drive up its winding streets reveals hardly a shade tree or a blade of grass along the way. We park near the single, squat tower that is all that is left of the castle of the once powerful Duke of Alba. I remember reading somewhere that the present Duchess of Alba has more titles after her name than the Queen of England.

We stroll up a long, narrow alley that, like much of the rest of Alba, still has a medieval feel to it. We emerge onto La Plaza de Santa Teresa, a slightly sloping rectangle bounded on four sides by tan stone buildings. Several ten-year-olds are charging recklessly over its cobblestones in a boisterous game of soccer. Weaving our way warily among the oblivious players we cross the rough pavement to the Carmelite Convent of the Annunciation and its adjacent Church of Santa Teresa.

After glancing for a few seconds at the almost windowless façade of the convent, we turn to our right and enter the church. At the far end looms an ornate main altar, flanked on either side by large gold-framed paintings. High above the altar table, behind wrought iron grillwork and sparkling in the glare of fluorescent lights, rests a black marble coffin surmounted by two white marble angels. Still higher up, almost at the ceiling, stands a statue of a Carmelite nun with a halo, her hands and eyes lifted in prayer toward heaven. This is Alba's main attraction: the tomb of Spain's most beloved saint, Teresa of Avila.

We join a small group of other visitors gathered at the altar rail around a tired old priest. He takes out a ring of keys that jangle as he unlocks a tiny compartment built into the wooden paneling to the left of the altar. Reverently pulling out a tall glass tube in a gold holder, he explains, "This is the actual heart of *la santa.*" Some of the visitors crowd closer to get a better look. Not me. "She died over 400 years ago, yet this heart is practically incorrupt." After feigning interest in the grisly relic for a few seconds, I start to look around at the rest of the quiet, peaceful church. It occurs to me that Teresa's life was anything but quiet and peaceful.

After some years and many spiritual struggles as a Carmelite nun in her native Avila, Teresa realized that her order was in dire need of reform. Despite being a woman in a man's world, she, with the help of Saint John of the Cross and others, began the difficult and thankless work of reforming the Carmelites; she founded several new houses, including this one in Alba de Tormes. Incredible as it sounds, all during this turmoil she was also writing some of the church's deepest and most enduring works on mystical prayer.

Teresa was a towering figure in her day, venerated by many as a saint while she was still alive. Within a few decades of her death the Catholic Church officially proclaimed her a saint, and in 1970 Pope Paul VI declared her a Doctor of the Church.

Many people admire the great saint's courage, others her deep mystical insights, and still others her remarkable personal holiness or her intense love for God and for humanity. The noble statue, the black marble sarcophagus, the sparkling silver and gold, all celebrate the importance of this towering historical figure: a courageous reformer, a great mystic, and a Doctor of the Church.

It occurs to me, though, as we follow the old priest to the back of the church, that there ought to be some reminder somewhere of a virtue of hers that is often overlooked: her heartfelt and intense humility. As Teresa began to receive great spiritual gifts from God, she also became more acutely aware of her unworthiness and her imperfections. Who was she, after all, she said to herself, that she should be receiving such divine gifts? Because she sincerely believed that everyone else was more virtuous than she was, Teresa never had a harsh word to say about anyone. In fact, she once insisted that her detractors were the only people who really knew her well. When her attempts to reform the Carmelite order attracted vicious, slanderous attacks from enemies who questioned even her chastity, she commented, "If they really knew me, they would say far worse things than that about me!" She always followed the spiritual advice she gave to her nuns: never make excuses when you are at fault, never grumble, and despise every mark of social rank or privilege.

Teresa's simple, down-to-earth realism and her deep sense of personal unworthiness seem forgotten amid the glittering gold, sparkling silver, polished marble, and elegant paintings in Alba de Tormes.

My thoughts are interrupted by Padre Angel, who is whispering to me "*¿Tienes dinero, no?* You have some money with you, don't you?" Our priest-guide is bidding us goodbye, and Padre Angel figures that I, being an *Americano*, can surely afford to give the old fellow a generous tip. I dutifully reach for my wallet.

As we head for the church door, I start thinking about Teresa's sense of playfulness. I recall reading that once she had her nuns stand up and dance for the Lord right in the chapel. I turn and look back down the long nave, imagining Teresa and her sisters tossing a white volleyball back and forth. Too bad no one has found a way to memorialize that side of her either, I think, as we step outside.

Whack! I'm startled by the loud crack of the soccer ball smacking solidly against the church wall. The boys, still totally engrossed in their game, barely notice the intruders sneaking across the middle of their field. A swarm of raucous shouts and flying elbows swoops past us chasing the white ball alongside the Church of Santa Teresa—the church wall is evidently considered in-bounds.

I suddenly realize that I have just discovered the missing piece of Teresa's memorial: the little Plaza de Santa Teresa itself, and the irreverent, boisterous game these noisy kids are playing in front of her convent. Yes! The simple sun-drenched plaza and the passionate soccer match counterbalance the cold, mute marble and the elegant gold of the church, completing the memorial to this very complex woman. I picture *la Santa* smiling down approvingly on the spirited boys from her perch high above the solemn, silent marble altar.

As we turn down the alley toward the car, Padre Angel asks with pride, "Well, what did you think? Pretty impressive, no?"

"*¡Si Padre, si!*" I answer.

Wham! Behind us, the ball whacks against the church wall.

"Yes, Padre Angel," I answer with a straight face, "it's a very fitting memorial for *la Santa*. Very fitting indeed!"

Reflection

During this first week of Lent we have been journeying with Jesus into the truth about ourselves, trying to see who we are in God's eyes, including both our strengths and our weaknesses—this is called humility. To many people humility is synonymous with self-hatred and "putting yourself down," the opposite of self-esteem. In fact, humility is simply the opposite of the illusion that I am perfect.

Teresa came to her deep sense of humility when she saw the tremendous gifts that God was giving her. Look at the specific gifts God has given you. Besides making you feel thankful, perhaps they can move you to a sense of how undeserving you are. Ask God to deepen your self-knowledge and grant you the gift of authentic humility.

Sacred Scripture (Luke 18:11–13, RSV)

The Pharisee stood and prayed thus with himself, "God, I thank thee that I am not like other men, extortioners, unjust, adulterers, or even like this tax collector. I fast twice a week, I give tithes of all that I get." But the tax collector, standing far off, would not even lift up his eyes to heaven, but beat his breast, saying, "God, be merciful to me a sinner!"

Rule of Benedict
(Chapter 4, "The Tools for Good Works," v. 62)

"Do not aspire to be called holy before you really are, but first be holy that you may more truly be called so."

Friday of the
First Week of Lent

Berlin, Germany:
Breaking Down Walls

Berlin's outdoor Christmas Market is in full swing. Scores of temporary wooden stalls line the crowded streets in the center of prosperous former West Berlin, and shoppers wander slowly from one to the next looking at the leather goods, sweaters, neckties, wood carvings, handmade jewelry, and plastic toys. They line up two deep at long outdoor bars that serve bratwurst and beer, or they stand in groups in front of stalls that advertise *Heisser Glühwein*, talking and drinking hot mulled wine. The city has a festive pre-Christmas atmosphere about it.

Reluctantly I turn from this scene to report for my guided tour of Berlin. Several other tourists are already on board the comfortable double-decker bus when I arrive. I settle in next to a window on the upper level and wait.

A tour of Berlin, more than of any other European city, is a quick trip through the history of the twentieth century. Berlin was intimately connected with the Prussia that was instrumental in unleashing World War I. She nurtured some of the most important movements in painting and literature. She witnessed the rise and fall of Adolph Hitler's Nazism, paying for it with her life's blood. She saw herself cut into two parts, like the world itself, by a wall that separated the Communist bloc from the "free world" of the West.

The bus rumbles into motion and the multilingual guide begins pointing out the important sights.

On your left is the Hauptbahnhof *or railroad station. . . . Also coming up on your left is the war memorial in the bombed-out ruins of the church called the Kaiser Kirche. It has been made into a shrine to pray for peace. . . . On your right you can see the Christmas Market. . . . Up ahead on your left is the city aquarium. . . . Across from the aquarium, notice the high-priced hotels for expense-account travelers, and the modern glass towers that are home to dozens of multinational corporations. . . .*

There's a feeling of busyness and prosperity on every side.

Ladies and gentlemen, we are now approaching what used to be the dividing line between "East Berlin" and "West Berlin." On your left you will see some remains of the Berlin Wall, and the guard post called "Checkpoint Charlie." The wall was begun on August 13th, 1961, and was torn down on November 9th, 1989. . . .

The bus rolls silently past a ragged, graffiti-covered stretch of the wall that has been left standing as a reminder of the twenty-eight years the city spent artificially divided into "East" and "West" Berlin. This ugly relic still has a sinister aura about it.

We rumble toward a large sign that once inspired fear but is now merely a curiosity for tourists. The driver slows down and twenty cameras point out of the left-side windows to click at the white signboard that warns ominously: "*ACHTUNG!* ATTENTION! You are now leaving the American-controlled sector of Berlin."

The bus rolls onward across the one-time border and into the former East Berlin. I'm shocked at the contrast. It's as if a color movie has just turned to black-and-white. The buildings are faceless, gray concrete cubes lined up along sad streets in monotonous rows. No anti-Communist propaganda film from the late fifties could do a better job of evoking the dismal mood of lifelessness and oppression.

That building on your right was the headquarters of the Soviet secret police. The one up ahead, on your left, is where political prisoners were taken for interrogation. . . .

A large gloomy field lies strangled by high weeds—in the center of the city! For the first time today, I notice how dark the clouds are overhead, and how chilly it looks out there.

We will now descend from the bus for ten minutes so that you may take photographs of the Brandenburg Gate. . . .

It's bitterly cold when I step out of the bus. I start sketching the gate but soon decide to climb back aboard and finish my work from the comfort of my warm seat by the window. The Brandenburg Gate fades in and out behind my breath condensing on the glass. My mind keeps being drawn back to that ominous section of the Wall.

One of the great tragedies of the dividing of Berlin into "East" and "West" was that relatives who happened to be living at different ends of town in August of 1961 suddenly found themselves on opposite sides of a wall with no way of reaching one another. If the call to be human is the call to be sister or brother to everyone else on the planet, then the Berlin Wall was a tragic parable in cinder block; it showed the world that any wall that cuts me off from another human being is cutting me off from a member of my family.

Jesus set us the example when he ignored the walls that the Jewish culture of his day had put up. He befriended women, lepers, prostitutes, tax-collectors, Samaritans, and other "outcasts" who were walled off from the accepted society of his day. In Benedict's time, rigid social distinctions were the normal way of life, but in his monasteries a Goth might find himself eating with a retired Roman soldier, and a scholar might be praying alongside an unlettered peasant.

If this bus tour is teaching me anything it's this: a wall that's meant to divide people is an ugly thing. Some individuals put up a Berlin wall in their heart with barbed wire on top, and consign whole groups to the other side of it because of skin color or nationality or religion. A subtle wall of fear, insecurity, or anger springs up when I quietly cut myself off from a particular person because of some injury or insult. I justify my behavior with the knowledge that I am right and the other person is wrong, and then, over time, I stop noticing how ugly the wall is; I come to accept the division as a normal part of my life. But no matter how it started, no matter if I am "right" or not, to the extent that this wall divides me from a brother or sister, it divides me from Jesus, who always identifies with the person on the other side of the wall.

Newsreels show the delirious joy of the Germans on the day the wall came down. The symbol of their dividedness had crumbled and left them standing on the pile of rubble and embracing their brothers and sisters from the other side of the wall. What a beautiful invitation to all humans to join in breaking down the world's walls wherever we find them!

Ladies and gentlemen, we will now continue our tour with a ride down the famous avenue called Unter den Linden. . . .

The linden trees are stark and bare in the dead of December. This whole part of the city looks as if it has been in the grip of winter for fifty years.

I promise myself to come back one day and visit Berlin in the summer. In the warm sunshine everything will look prettier—everything except the Wall.

Reflection

Lent's call to repentance challenges us to look for things that are separating us from Christ. Take some time to reflect on the walls you may have erected in your heart that separate you from a particular person or group. (Remember that certain walls may have become such familiar parts of the landscape over time that they may be hard to spot.) Picture that wall: what is it made of? Does it look old or new? Is it pretty or ugly? Is it solid or crumbling? How does the wall make you feel: Comfortable? Safe? Sad?

Ask the Lord if there is something you could do about that wall during this Lenten season.

Sacred Scripture (Eph. 2:13–14, RSV)

"But now in Christ Jesus you who once were far off have been brought near in the blood of Christ. For he is our peace, who has made us both one, and has broken down the dividing wall of hostility."

Rule of Benedict
(Chapter 2, "Qualities of the Abbot," vv. 16–20)

The abbot should avoid all favoritism in the monastery. He is not to love one more than another unless he finds someone better in good actions and obedience. A man born free is not to be given higher rank than a slave who becomes a monk, except for some good reason. But the abbot is free, if he sees fit, to change anyone's rank as justice demands. Ordinarily, everyone is to keep his regular place, because whether slave or free, we are all one in Christ.

Saturday of the First Week of Lent

Saint Julien le Pauvre, Paris: Letting Go of Perfection

With its rough stone walls and low Romanesque lines, it looks like a village church that has lost its way and wandered, bewildered, into one of the noisiest neighborhoods of Paris. Just across the river from the great Gothic towers of Notre Dame, I step through a modest doorway into the dimly lit Church of Saint Julien le Pauvre.

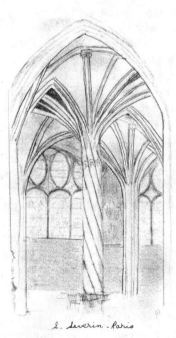

S. Severin - Paris

It still keeps the humble simplicity it had when it served as a shrine for medieval pilgrims on their way to Compostela. In recent years, its charming, intimate interior has made the church a popular spot for chamber music concerts.

I find a seat in the second row—my reward for coming early—and glance over the evening's printed program. I recognize the titles of several familiar pieces by Mozart, Vivaldi, and Handel. There is still plenty of time to gaze around and take in the scene.

The simple round arches, dark vaults, and small windows give me the sense of closeness that I've felt in little parish churches in farming towns. Recently, Saint Julien was assigned to the Greek Melkite Church as their regular worship space, and so a colorful iconostasis—a wooden partition decorated with hand-painted icons—has

41

been built across the front of the apse and hung with flickering votive candles. This adds a touch of life and color to the otherwise somber beauty of the place. In the narrow, brightly lit area between this altar screen and the front row of the audience, eight empty chairs face outward and wait self-consciously for the members of the string ensemble to make their appearance.

My imagination fills the church with pilgrims passing through, as they used to do in the middle ages, on their way to Compostela. I can almost hear the church's bell ring out as it did for centuries to call the students to their classes at the nearby Sorbonne.

From the rear of the church, a ripple of applause grows to a wave as the musicians, clad in traditional black-and-white formal dress, walk briskly down the left aisle and take their seats in the sanctuary. The first violinist will also act as conductor of the group. There is a final muted tune-up, then a couple of seconds of pregnant silence. Finally the instruments burst into a robust rendition of Mozart's *Eine Kleine Nachtmusik*.

"Bomp, ba-bomp, ba-bomp ba-bomp ba-BOMP!" The young man playing the bass violin is obviously enjoying himself, his expressive face letting everyone know that this is one of his favorite pieces. The young violist, on the other hand, plays precisely; her only goal seems to be technical perfection. The woman to her right, with short brown hair, looks as though she loves playing, but seems a little bit tired. I wonder if she's a mother who has had to hire a babysitter for the evening, and has left the supper dishes in the sink. The unkempt first violinist has a lot of the showman about him and conducts by swinging the far end of his violin in expansive circles. I look once again at the bass player. For the last few moments he has not been playing, but simply standing with his eyes closed, nodding his approval of the violin passage and smiling at the little surprises that Mozart slips in now and then.

The second movement already, the andante: "Da, da, DAH . . . dee DAH-da DAH-da DAH-da-DAH!" The first violinist is now conducting by drawing acrobatic figure eights with the scroll-end of his instrument while never missing a note.

I seldom get to attend chamber music concerts when I'm home in the monastery, but have to content myself with recordings of the great artists and orchestras on CDs or on some FM station. There really is something special about a live performance. First, of course, there is the sense of human contact as you get to know the lively bass player, the young mother with the viola, and the showman on first violin. But even more gratifying than getting to know the musicians is the presence of something you never hear on a compact disc recording at home: imperfections!

These performers in front of me are professionals, and they're good. Every now and then, however, maybe just once in a whole concert, somebody will hit a couple of muddy notes that should have been sparkling diamonds. Hrumph! complains the little critic inside of me. On my recording at home, Bruno Walter and the Columbia Symphony Orchestra do a much better job on that passage!

Oh! Here's the third movement, the allegretto: "Da-DUMP-dum, dah DAH; da DUMP dump, dah DA-da DA-da Da-da. . . ." The bass violinist sticks the tip of his tongue out of the corner of his mouth as he concentrates on moving his fingers nimbly through a particularly delicious bass run. Suddenly he breaks into a broad smile as if he's just remembered a good joke.

As I watch and listen, it dawns on me that what I hear on a digital CD is usually a thoroughly sanitized performance. There are no friendly background noises of squeaking chairs and stifled coughs. All the imperfections have been removed electronically, all the poor passages redone, and every blemish cosmetically removed by clever audio engineers.

No fancy audio tricks here in Saint Julien tonight, though. These musicians are real people who have families and friends. They eat lunch, smoke cigarettes, take the mètro, and discuss politics like everybody else. Each of them contributes his or her talent to the group, and together they are making the stone vaults ring with the heavenly harmonies of Mozart. They play quite well together, no doubt about it. Still, this is a group of human beings, so they're not perfect.

None of them seems preoccupied with being perfect, either, with the possible exception of the violist—the one with her black hair pulled back in a tight bun. I study her stern face for a moment and start to feel vaguely uneasy. Suddenly I realize why I don't like that forbidding but familiar expression: It's *my* face, my "work" face. Whenever I do a job, my unconscious goal is always to do it perfectly. It is, needless to say, a bit of a strain on coworkers and brother monks, and on me, too. During this year away, I'm getting a chance to step back from my perfectionism and look at it from the outside, the way I'm looking at this violist. And I don't like what I see.

The fourth and last movement of *Eine Kleine*, the allegro. They're really moving this one along: "DRRRIN-din, din-din, DUNT-dunt-Dun!" The young bassist is throwing himself body and soul into the marvelous bass line, so "into" the music that he's playing it from the inside out. He's so uplifted and enthralled by the beauty of what the group is creating up there that he has left any concerns about perfection far, far behind.

Beauty and harmony are goals that are within our reach, but perfection is not—that's reserved for God alone. This is why Benedict's vision for his community is not perfection but peace and harmony. He strictly forbids grumbling, and often recommends some course of action "so that no one be saddened in the house of God" or "that no one be given a justifiable reason for complaint." He knows that monks are imperfect, but he holds out to them the challenge to build a "peaceable kingdom" in the monastery.

These imperfect musicians who still make such beautiful music together remind me that I don't need to be a perfect Christian, a perfect monk, or a perfect anything else. I just need to concentrate on making music with my brothers and sisters in the monastery and in our school, music that isn't perfect—only beautiful.

In a flash of insight I see the truth about myself: I am a recovering perfectionist. I immediately promise myself to attend these concerts faithfully, hoping vaguely that these musicians will be a support group. As the audience breaks into heartfelt applause, the musicians stand and acknowledge our enthusiasm. I'm already looking forward to our next meeting.

Reflection

What is your attitude as you keep Lent? Do you go about it with the grim determination of the scowling perfectionist on the viola, or perhaps with the joy of the ebullient bassist? Benedict expects us during Lent to "look forward to holy Easter with joy and spiritual longing."

Fasting and prayer help to foster harmony within you by taming wayward desires and keeping your priorities in proper order. This inner peace then overflows into the rest of your life. Ask yourself how well you foster harmony with the people around you. Think of an area where you may be a source of discord. How might you change that?

Sacred Scripture (Ps. 34:14)

"Seek peace, and pursue it."

Rule of Benedict
(Chapter 72, "The Good Zeal of Monks," vv. 4–6)

"They should each try to be the first to show respect to the other, supporting with the greatest patience one another's weaknesses of body or behavior, and earnestly competing in obedience to one another."

THE SECOND WEEK OF LENT

Holy Combat

In the wilderness the Israelites were constantly doing battle: against external enemies such as the hostile Amalekites, against internal ones such as discouragement and temptations to idolatry. In the middle ages a pilgrimage was an arduous and dangerous enterprise—sometimes even fatal. Violence was always a possibility, whether from highway robbers, from criminals posing as fellow pilgrims, or from warring armies.

In the deserts of northern Egypt the monastic fathers and mothers used to speak of the spiritual life as "sacred warfare," in which the enemy was the devil and the battleground the human heart. The meditations this week explore the image of holy combat from various angles. "Eger" warns us to watch for the enemy within. "Waterloo" asks us to make a healthy critique of the influences in our culture that can weaken our commitment to the gospel. "Arles" and "Toledo" challenge us to free ourselves from those "negligences" that Benedict speaks of in his chapter on Lent. "Fulda" urges us to set about the task right away, since none of us knows how much time we have left on the journey. Finally, "Saint Etienne" encourages us to go about the Christian combat with a spirit of confident optimism.

Monday of the Second Week of Lent

Eger, Hungary:
Watching for the Enemy Within

A blistering August sun makes the climb feel steeper than it really is. As we trudge up a dusty approach road to the ruins at the top of this hill in northeastern Hungary, one of my three Hungarian hosts, a retired schoolteacher, tells me the story of the heroes of the siege of Eger. Every Hungarian schoolchild knows it.

During the summer of 1552, two Turkish armies had already captured thirty Hungarian strongholds with little trouble, and figured to take the fortress of Eger just as easily. As we reach the entrance gate at the top, it's clear why the Turks expected to make short work of it. Eger is in a poor strategic position: hills rise above its eastern and northern sides, offering attackers perfect placements for short-range guns and a view of everything going on inside the walls below. And yet, the Hungarian commander, István Dobo, and his two thousand brave men and women held off forty thousand Turks on this spot for thirty-nine gruesome days, persevering until the frustrated attackers simply gave up and went home in disgrace. The heroic deeds of the defenders have been retold ever since in poetry, story, and song.

We pass through the gate and onto a dusty field surrounded by low stone walls and a few reconstructed buildings. I can feel that this is indeed a sacred site, a place baptized in blood.

During that famous siege in the summer of 1552 the sandstone walls were pounded into rubble by enemy cannons, but enough of the ruins remain to give my imagination plenty to play with. We stand on the north wall looking across a quiet little ravine at the facing hill that once swarmed with turbaned Turkish soldiers. It's as if the siege guns have just stopped their constant booming, and there is an eerie hush before the next attack. . . .

Here they come! Wave upon wave of *janissaries, saabs, delis,* and *djebedjis,* screaming "*Allah akbar*" as they storm the walls, trying to plant their red pennants on the ramparts. Clouds of choking black smoke belch from cannons and rifles. The ingenious exploding devices of Gergeley Bornemissza start spewing fire and death, sowing panic in the ranks of the Turks.

The desperate Hungarian defenders have already beaten off several frenzied assaults, and enemy corpses are beginning to pile up at the foot of Eger's ramparts. So the wily Turkish commander has added another tactic: his men are digging a tunnel under the walls, planning to come up inside the stronghold and catch the Hungarians by surprise. But here in the fort, commander Dobo, being no stranger to such tricks himself, suspects that the Turks are burrowing beneath the walls of Eger. And he has a solution: all the way around the inside of the wall, at set intervals, he places simple peasant bowls filled with water to act as detectors. Each time a sentry comes to one of these bowls he will stop and watch the surface of the water for telltale ripples.

A few days later a breathless guard races up to his commanding officer, "Sir! Come quickly! The bowl in the stable! The water's moving!" They crowd into the empty stall and lean over the peasant bowl to watch excitedly. Sure enough, there in the flickering torch light, tiny ripples, too small to notice without staring, are making ominous rings in the water. Those little waves tell of a deadly scheme unfolding under their very feet. Deep beneath the wall of the fortress, the Turks are busy tunneling. The hapless diggers, planning a surprise attack, will now get a deadly shock themselves when they finally break through.

I can think of a few times when I've been caught completely off guard by some totally unexpected outburst of my own pettiness or plain nastiness. I've seen more than one person burst out in a fit of childish anger or cruel selfishness and then look around, appalled at the wreckage they've just caused, and ask themselves, "Where did *that* come from?" If I don't want to be taken by surprise by my emotions and inner drives, I can learn a lesson from the heroes of Eger, whose sentries kept a careful eye on those bowls of water placed on the ground. I have my own bowls that bear watching, signals that reveal to me something of my inner life: maybe a certain passing emotion, or an unpleasant run-in with someone, or an over-reaction to some trivial problem.

Of course I may be justified in being a little upset at finding that someone's put an empty cereal box back in the cupboard, but this time the petty annoyance triggers a burst of furious anger. Suddenly an image flashes in front of me: a bowl of water is sitting on the dirt floor of a fortress, and on the surface of the water are tiny disturbances. Like those ripples that were barely visible but gave a valuable warning about what was happening underneath the fortress of Eger, my outburst is a very useful tip-off: I need to ask myself what is really bothering me—something deeper, at work beneath the surface of my life. Maybe an incident that happened yesterday in a meeting or some bad news about a close friend last night upset me more than I realized. My flare-up becomes both a useful warning and a clear challenge to unearth the real but hidden issue and deal with it somehow.

The Hungarian sentry had been taught the meaning of the ripples in the water and was on the watch for them. We, too, have our own bowls of water, and like that sentry, we can make use of them in our spiritual combat. They can alert us if, beneath the calm surface of our lives, there is an unseen problem that demands attention. They can make us aware of some unpleasant truth about ourselves that we've been reluctant to face.

"Well, are you ready to go? We're all getting hot and tired." The schoolteacher's words bring me out of my musing with a jolt.

The heat is now rising up from the dust in heavy sheets. My friends and I agree that it's time to call it quits. Hot and exhausted, we trudge back down the long road the way we came, like the tired Turks of 1552.

Reflection

Lent is traditionally seen as a desert season, a time for spiritual combat. Think of what this may mean for you. If Benedict refers several times to fighting the spiritual combat, he writes even more often about being vigilant, making watchfulness one of the fundamental attitudes to be cultivated in the monastery. *Lectio divina* and honest, introspective prayer are just two of the practices that can help us to look into our own hearts.

What are the "bowls of water" in your life, that is, feelings and actions that usually warn you that something more may be going on inside you?

Sacred Scripture (1 Cor. 16:13–14, RSV)

"Be watchful, stand firm in your faith, be courageous, be strong. Let all that you do be done in love."

Rule of Benedict (Chapter 7, "Humility," v. 29)

"Then, brothers, we must be vigilant every hour or, as the Prophet says in the psalm, God may observe us falling at some time into evil."

Tuesday of the
Second Week of Lent

Waterloo, Belgium:
Checking the Visitors

The night is as black as licorice. Sitting alone in a compartment of the Amsterdam-to-Paris train, I click off the overhead lamp and start watching mysterious pinpoints of light slide past outside. We rumble through little stations whose darkened windows stare blankly, like great blind eyes. We're crossing Belgium, that favorite corridor for armies charging back and forth between France and Germany. The constant clacking rhythm of the wheels on the rails lulls me to sleep in my seat.

I hear distant cannon fire and the whinnying of terrified horses, echoes of the desperate battles of 1914 in the Ardennes forest way off to the east. The sharp smell of gunpowder wafts across the hills.

The rhythm of the wheels slows, and I wake up as a weird glare comes pouring through the window and floods my compartment with an unnatural glow. I hold my hands in front of me; they're pale blue. We've pulled into the station of some large city. Let's see . . . we've already passed Antwerp, so this is probably Brussels. Several quiet figures stand on the concrete platform under the fluorescent lights watching the train come to a stop. There's always something sad about travelers waiting in a station in the middle of the night. The muffled sound of their voices comes through the window. There are a couple of anonymous thumps out in the corridor as suitcases bump against the walls. A shrill whistle from the conductor, and a moment later we glide out of the station. The wheels set up their monotonous clacking again; in a few minutes they'll take us past the town of Waterloo. I doze off.

Napoleon's troops are already scurrying about, preparing for a charge across a flat plain at first light. Drums roll, calling the soldiers to form ranks behind their banners. In the morning mist the Duke of Wellington's English are already awaiting the fateful attack.

I sense a human presence in the compartment with me. I half open my eyes to see a man in a suit and tie sitting in the shadows on the opposite side of the dark compartment, just inside the sliding door. Funny, he came in without making a sound. My senses are dull with sleep, and my head is heavy on my shoulders. Soon my cheek rests once again against the rough cloth of the window curtain and my eyelids droop closed.

The battle trumpet sounds, the drums pound, and the attack begins. The French troops charge across the wide field. Horses snort and neigh in the heat of battle. The cannons belch death and mutilation; Napoleon's charge starts to falter.

I sense that presence again, but nearer this time. I open my eyes a little and am startled to see that the man in the suit is now standing just a few inches away from me, to my right, his arms stretching up over my head. His hands are busy on the luggage shelf above me.

The little part of my brain that doesn't go to sleep on trains gives the rest of me a poke and asks, "Why is this man standing here reaching up to the overhead rack where your blazer is?" In an instant my eyes are wide open. I tilt my head up toward the dark form hovering above me and ask in polite, sleepy French, "*M'sieur? Je peux vous aider?* Can I help you, sir?" He doesn't answer, but instead just calmly turns to his left, takes two or three steps back to his corner seat by the door and sits down. My eyelids close once more. . . .

I hear a familiar sound: the door to the corridor is slowly sliding shut. The corner seat is empty, and I'm alone in the compartment again. As the clouds clear from my brain, I start to realize that my visitor had been going through my coat pockets looking for my wallet!

I'm not awake enough to be angry at him, but I have to admire his nerve. Then I start to scold myself for not being more aware that something unusual was afoot. This stranger shows up in my compartment looking for a seat at 2:00 a.m., a full half-hour after we had left the last station. How could I have been so slow to pick up on that?

Finally I end up feeling insulted. Did that guy really think that I would be dumb enough to leave anything of value lying around where some sleazy stranger could just sneak in and snatch it? In fact, when I'm on a night train, I always put my passport, wallet, and tickets in my back pocket and sit on them. (This is not very comfortable, but it's highly effective.) The thief, then, never had the slightest chance of stealing anything of value from me. Now wide awake, I start thinking—you need to be conscious of who's in the compartment with you.

We don't need to be paranoid, of course; but we do need to be watchful. Benedictines, for example, have a well-deserved reputation for hospitality, but the *Rule* actually shows a marked distrust of guests. As soon as one shows up at the door, the superior and the brothers must always pray with the guest before exchanging the kiss of peace, "because of the delusions of the devil." Brothers are not to speak with a guest without the abbot's permission. Experience had shown Benedict that, like my night visitor, evil influences can sometimes slip into the monastery unnoticed—forces that can slowly erode our commitment to living the gospel.

This is true for any Christian trying to follow Christ. Take, for instance, the influence of mass media. TV sitcoms and junk magazines slip into our homes in the guise of innocent relaxation, and soon become familiar friends. It's curious how we protect ourselves from harmful intruders by putting double locks on our doors and burglar alarms on our windows, but then we allow into our homes a parade of seedy strangers in rented movies and television programs—strangers who pose a real threat to our deepest beliefs and convictions. Constant and indiscriminate exposure to programs that glorify materialism, deceit, selfishness, and promiscuity will inevitably change our attitudes, confuse our sense of right and wrong, and weaken our determination to follow Christ. To think otherwise is simply naïve.

No, I'm far from alone in my train compartment. Lots of characters are passing in and out all the time—and some of them bear careful watching. On the long night's journey to the Kingdom there has to be a part of me that doesn't go to sleep, that keeps asking questions: "Why am I watching this program that glorifies adultery?" "Do I really need this item I'm about to buy, or have I been talked into it by advertisers?" I have to keep shooing off the well-dressed night visitors: "*Pardon. Je peux vous aider?* Excuse me, can I help you?"

Lines of German Panzer tanks are rolling past my window to join the furious fighting far off to the east. It's 1944, and General Dwight Eisenhower's troops are digging in for a fight to the death. History will call it "The Battle of the Bulge." Clouds of oily black smoke billow from burning towns on the horizon. It's as if the eastern sky itself were on fire. . . .

Then I realize that the red in the sky is the sunrise; the smoke is the city smog hanging over the outskirts of Paris. I stand up and stretch my arms over my head with a short grunt, swaying as the train clatters and lurches on its final few miles. I notice, just above eye-level, my navy blue blazer lying in its place on the rack. My right hand reaches back instinctively to tap my pants pocket. I smile smugly as I feel my passport and wallet still safe where they belong.

Outside the window the distant white domes of Sacré Coeur Basilica glow pink in the dawn over Paris.

Reflection

Lent is a good time to scrutinize the "strangers" you may have invited to walk with you on your life's pilgrimage through television programs, reading material, and Internet sites. Look carefully at a few of these, one at a time, and ask them some questions: "Did I consciously invite you along, or did you just sneak in?" "Are you heading toward the same goal as I am?" "Just how are you helping me on my journey to the Kingdom?" You might try "fasting" from certain television programs or other forms of entertainment during Lent.

Sacred Scripture (1 Pet. 5:8–9, RSV)

"Be sober, be watchful. Your adversary the devil prowls around like a roaring lion, seeking some one to devour. Resist him, firm in your faith."

Rule of Benedict
(Chapter 53, "The Reception of Guests," vv. 3–5)

"Once a guest has been announced, the superior and the brothers are to meet him with all the courtesy of love. First of all, they are to pray together and thus be united in peace, but prayer must always precede the kiss of peace because of the delusions of the devil."

Wednesday of the Second Week of Lent

Arles, France:
Letting God Shine Through

I park my rented car in a lot near the ancient Roman arena in Arles and set off on foot through the narrow, picturesque streets. This delightful town of gray stone buildings and orange tile roofs was once the starting point for the southernmost of the four great pilgrimage routes through France to Compostela. It is best known though, for its well-preserved Roman ruins.

Cloître ~ S. Trophime, Arles

Located at the delta where the Rhone empties into the Mediterranean, Arelatae, as the Romans called it, was once the second capital of the Roman world. The partially restored amphitheater and the coliseum-like arena are both still used for special events today. Their immense size and sober dignity are a pleasant contrast to the lighthearted spirit of present-day Arles.

It was in a college art class that I first saw pictures of the lovely carved portal that graces the front of the church of Saint Trophime, one of the great treasures of Romanesque architecture. This morning I'm finally going to be able to just stand there and marvel at it with my own eyes. Then, right beside the church, there will be the famous cloister garden, the most beautiful one in southern France.

Arriving at last in the wide, stone-paved Place de la République, I immediately turn to my left, toward the church of Saint Trophime. After a wait of more than thirty years, I am finally able to stand here in person and look up at—four stories of scaffolding! The famous carved Romanesque doorway is completely hidden behind ugly panels of corrugated steel! I stand and stare in angry disbelief for a few moments, and then, heavy with disappointment, I shuffle halfheartedly into the church.

Since it's not yet nine o'clock in the morning, I have it all to myself. I sit and pray for a while in the quiet glow of the early sun beneath towering twelfth-century vaults topped with rounded Romanesque arches. My guidebook calls the interior "the high point of Romanesque church architecture." I turn the page and look wistfully at a color photograph of the famous portal that I won't get to see. It's a set of pillars arranged like a triumphal arch, symbolizing the entrance of the People of God into the Heavenly Jerusalem. It includes beautifully carved stone statues of saints and, in the semicircular tympanum above the main doors, the famous scene of "Christ in Judgment." I have to admit that even in this flattering photograph the whole thing is blackened and filthy with the soot of centuries. I imagine how glorious it will look after a good cleaning.

I walk out of the church through the forest of scaffold pipes and plywood panels and back onto the plaza. A few yards to the left, I step through a gate and into Saint Trophime's cloister garden. I sense right away the gentle peacefulness of the place, a sort of timeless hush, as if the pewter-colored stones were absorbing all the sounds of the world. I follow the arcaded stone walkway that surrounds the square patch of bright green lawn. On two of the four sides Romanesque columns with squat little sculptures on the capitals support rounded arches. Along the other two sides the pointed gothic arches display carvings that are more intricate and elegant. The cloister garden keeps the easy quietness it had when the canons of Saint Trophime, who followed the Rule of Saint Augustine, used this as their place of meditation and prayer.

I sit down on a stone bench and take out a photocopy of a Latin sermon written by Caesarius of Arles, a favorite saint of mine. I've brought it all the way from my monastery back home just so I can sit here and enjoy it in the town where it was written. Caesarius was bishop here for forty years around the year 500 A.D., long before this church or cloister were built. He had been a monk of the monastery of Lérins on the island of Saint Honorat near Cannes, but then was sent here to Arles to be its bishop. He became famous as a preacher, a theologian, and a saint.

I unfold the pages. As I start to read the sermon, which has traveled so far to come back to its home, a gentle breeze rustles the leaves in some nearby shrubs. As usual, Caesarius' Latin is not the richly ornate language of Augustine (which I find too hard to read), but is deliberately simple and homespun, intended to reach the common people.

This sermon turns out to be on one of his favorite subjects: the dangers posed by "little" sins, those trivial faults that are a normal part of daily life. One reason they're dangerous, the bishops argues, is that we are in a battle with an enemy; there's no room for letting down our guard. People who figure that they're safe because they don't have any grave sins are likely to get overconfident. "It is exactly at this point that they get seriously wounded because they are not expecting the attack."

"Some of you," the Caesarius continues, "are misled into thinking that just because you never do anything evil, God will surely judge you worthy of everlasting life." I think of the elegant carving of Christ in Judgment that is hidden by the workmen's scaffold. "Well, let me remind you of Jesus' parable about the last judgment: the tree gets cut down and thrown into the fire not for bearing *bad* fruit but for bearing *no* fruit." In other words, if you haven't been about the business of bearing the fruit of love and forgiveness then you'd better start right now!

Caesarius shows his characteristic impatience with people who are satisfied with just being "pretty good," who have made a friendly truce with their daily faults and petty vices. I squirm a bit on the hard bench as he brings up the example of Ananias who was struck dead for holding back just a small part of what he had promised to give to the Lord. God isn't interested in having most of what I have—God wants it all.

I remember another sermon, in which the monk-bishop points out to some monks how illogical it is to give up all the pleasures of the world in order to follow Christ in the monastic life, and then, once in the monastery, be only lukewarm or half-hearted about it. Before being appointed a bishop, Caesarius had been the "cellarer" of the monastery of Lérins, in charge of distributing supplies and daily necessities to the monks. Some say he was removed from that job because he was too strict in dealing with his brethren. After reading his sermons, I can believe it.

Blackbirds dart and swoop in tight circles, playing an irreverent game of tag above the dusty orange tiles of the church roof.

Caesarius' relentless demands for holiness, however, spring from this fundamental optimistic belief: we are made in the image of God. The image is often tarnished or caked with layers of "*parvas negligentias quotidianas,"* daily little faults. After years of neglect, it can get to be so covered over as to be unrecognizable. I think of the blackened portal of Saint Trophime nearby. Removing those layers and letting our true self shine through takes constant care and the regular practice of prayer, penance, and almsgiving. I may be satisfied with leaving a little dirt on the image, but my bishop friend clearly is not. He would remind me that I can do much better—after all, I am the image of God.

When I finish reading I fold up the pages of the sermon and tuck them back into my knapsack. Reluctantly, I stand up and stretch, squinting into the warm summer sun. I say a quiet good-bye to the gray stone arches, the lush green grass, and the tranquil silence and then step quietly out of the cloister garden.

Back again in the busy Place de la République, I pass in front of the scaffold hiding the church; I hear the voices of the workers who are painstakingly removing centuries of dirt. After several more months all of the images on the façade will be restored to their original beauty, thanks to the thorough cleaning. Yes, I think to myself, Caesarius would definitely approve.

Reflection

The *Rule of Benedict* urges us "to wash away in this holy season the negligences of other times." What are some things that are covering over the image of God in you? How might certain Lenten practices help remove them? Pray that you may live in such a way that others can see the image of God in you.

Sacred Scripture (Col. 3:9–10, RSV)

"Do not lie to one another, seeing that you have put off the old nature with its practices and have put on the new nature, which is being renewed in knowledge after the image of its creator."

Rule of Benedict
(Chapter 49, "The Observance of Lent," vv. 2–4)

"We urge the entire community during these days of Lent to keep its manner of life most pure and to wash away in this holy season the negligences of other times. This we can do in a fitting manner by refusing to indulge evil habits and by devoting ourselves to prayer with tears, to reading, to compunction of heart and self-denial."

Thursday of the Second Week of Lent

Toledo, Spain:
Breaking Chains

I'm strolling toward the old part of Toledo from the bus terminal well outside the ancient walls. In A.D. 123 Titus Livy described Toledo as "a small fortified city." Since that time, it has changed hands among Romans, Visigoths, Moslems, and Spanish monarchs, but on this spring morning as I approach the city gate, Toledo still keeps its air of "a small fortified city."

I recognize the skyline from the famous painting, "Storm Over Toledo," El Greco's almost mystical vision of the cathedral on the hilltop, its gray tower pointing into the shreds of black and silver cloud as vibrant green fields in the foreground climb upward toward the purplish gray city walls. Passing through the medieval gate, I climb the ramparts. After a few minutes of gazing down at the Tagus River winding across the rolling farmland, I set off to explore the town's narrow streets.

I wander through quiet old neighborhoods whose houses bear the stamp of 360 years of Moslem rule, and busy commercial areas with their window displays of beautiful silver work and famous Toledo cutlery. After stopping at the house where El Greco did some of his most famous paintings, I come to one of the largest gothic structures in the world. Toledo's cathedral has five naves; the central and tallest one, supported by eighty-eight pillars, towers 150 feet above the floor. Everywhere there are masterpieces of painting and sculpture, of gold and silver work. After an hour of visiting I decide my feet need a rest, and I head for the door.

Some blocks later I find myself in a wide sun-bathed plaza alongside the monastery church of San Juan de los Reyes. High up on an outside wall, hanging in neat rows, are curious ironwork objects about a foot-and-a-half long. Grateful for the excuse to sit down, I find a bench in the shade and consult my guidebook to find out what those things are. A few seconds of page-turning solves the mystery: these are ankle chains taken off of Christian slaves freed from the Moslems by the victorious

Spaniards in 1492. I stare at these grisly reminders of slavery, and try to hear the story they tell of slaves being set free from captivity and returning joyfully to their homes and families.

It strikes me that the side of a church is the perfect place to display the broken chains of Christians who once were held captive. Our God is, after all, in the business of breaking chains. We believe that the Word became flesh, suffered, died, and rose again to free us from the chains of sin and death. We are no longer slaves to evil, doubt, and despair, because the Lord has loosed our bonds.

As I watch the wall of San Juan de los Reyes glow in the afternoon sun, it easily becomes the wall of my own abbey church. The rusting Moslem leg irons suddenly belong not to anonymous slaves, but to me and my brother monks back home. The broken shackles become souvenirs of temptations we've overcome, trophies of little triumphs over vices, the tally of the times Jesus' saving power has set one of us free.

What if we could see trophies like this displayed on every church wall in the world? What if every victory over the fetters of pettiness and jealousy, for example, were recorded by hanging up the broken chains somewhere as an encouragement for the rest of us? What if we could actually see and count up the hundreds, thousands, and millions of times that Jesus has delivered someone's heart from the slavery of pride, hatred, or racial prejudice? What if the walls of drug and alcohol treatment centers could display to the world the broken bonds of addictions overcome? What if houses, apartment buildings, and convents were decked with the rusty remains of misunderstandings that have been overcome by love, courage, and God's grace? What an encouragement that would be to people who find themselves struggling with weaknesses, sins, or addictions! The display of shattered chains in front of me this afternoon prompts me to steal a glance at my own personal chains—the broken ones and the unbroken.

It's time to step back out of El Greco's Toledo and into the reality of evening traffic and long lines at the bus station. On my walk down the hill, I spot another church, but there are no chains on the wall. I start looking for them everywhere: on houses, storefronts, and police stations. I can almost see one, I think, hanging in the shadows underneath that balcony, where an old woman is sitting in the doorway watching the sun go down.

Reflection

What are some personal chains (habits, feelings, ways of thinking, etc.) that are weighing you down on your journey? Choose one in particular and reflect on how it is holding you back. Do you really want to be free of it? If so, ask the Lord to help you. Perhaps there is a particular step you can offer to take in this regard as part of your Lenten observance?

If there is a chain that has been a problem for a long time, you might try this prayer: "Lord, if it is your will that I drag this chain along as Jesus carried his cross, then I will keep dragging it; please give me the strength to do so graciously. But on the other hand, if it is not your will that I drag this chain around, if you want me to be free of it, that would be fine with me, but you have to do the freeing, because I can't do it by myself."

Sacred Scripture (Acts 12:6–7, RSV)

The very night when Herod was about to bring him out, Peter was sleeping between two soldiers, bound with two chains, and sentries before the door were guarding the prison; and behold, an angel of the Lord appeared, and a light shone in the cell; and he struck Peter on the side and woke him, saying, "Get up quickly." And the chains fell off his hands.

Rule of Benedict (Chapter 5, "Obedience," v. 12)

"[Monks] no longer live by their own judgment, giving in to their whims and appetites; rather they walk according to another's decisions and directions, choosing to live in monasteries and to have an abbot over them."

Friday of the
Second Week of Lent

Fulda, Germany:
Being Prepared

The snow outside is rushing past the train window in those tiny flakes that promise a lot more to come. Central Germany is covered with a white blanket three inches deep. The table in front of me is covered with my things: paperback book, breviary, notebook, travel guides, and a small bag of pretzels. Buried under the debris is a single sheet of paper provided by the German railroad company, listing the time of arrival for each town, as well as the main connecting trains that can be met at each of the stations on our route. We've just pulled in for a three-minute stop at Fulda.

I peer out the window into the cottony whiteness and can't see much of anything. But my mind's eye goes to work with no trouble—the name Fulda evokes all sorts of history for a Benedictine.

I imagine I can see the cathedral built originally as the Benedictine abbey church in the early 1700s. Then there is the monastery itself, which became famous when Saint Boniface, "the Apostle of Germany," lived here as a monk for ten years before his martyrdom in 754. In the next century the abbey would grow to more than four hundred monks, and would boast a renowned *scriptorium* and an influential monastery school. For three hundred years, it was the most important imperial abbey in Germany, producing masterpieces in manuscript illumination and murals, in gold work and sculpture.

I stop staring out at the snow, and my eye wanders down to the table in front of me. I notice the corner of the train schedule peeking out from under my red pencil case. I pull it out and start to read it in an absent-minded way. Let's see. . . . Here we are, Fulda—right on time. There are even a couple of connecting trains you can catch at Fulda. Hmm! An express train for Munich comes in five minutes, and arrives in Munich at 5:30 p.m. That's funny, that sounds like the time I'm planning to get there myself. I need to catch the 6 o'clock train from Munich to Plattling.

Suddenly I get an uneasy feeling in the pit of my stomach—something's not right here. . . .

My eyes jump quickly to the bottom of the sheet, and I gasp when I see that this train that I'm on gets into Munich at 7:05—an hour too late! The awful truth hits me like a fist: I'm supposed to change trains here at Fulda. I've got to get off this train and onto the other one!

I start shoving everything from the tabletop into my knapsack. Pencils, prayer book, paperback, and pretzels all vanish with a sweep of a hand. I'm on my feet, shrugging into my blazer while pulling my suitcase and my winter coat from the overhead rack. I have to get off the train before it pulls out! Any second now it'll start to move, and I'll be in a real mess. With barely a glance at my empty place to see if I've left anything behind, I stagger up the aisle toward the nearest exit. I toss my suitcase ahead of me into the entryway by the open door, hoping that the conductor outside will realize that there's still someone planning to get off. I'm in the vestibule looking down at the conductor who is standing peacefully on the platform, his breath making big puffs of steam in the frosty air. Clutching my suitcase and my knapsack with its half-open zipper, I clamber down the steep steps squeezing my overcoat under one elbow, its collar dragging at my ankles.

I step noiselessly onto the cushion of new snow that carpets the little station platform and ask the conductor if there is indeed an express for Munich due in here in five minutes. "*Ja wohl!*" he assures me. Right on this same track, in fact. I just have to stand right where I am for a few minutes. I thank him as he signals the engineer that all is ready and climbs back up through the doorway. The snow-speckled train glides silently away from the station to continue its journey without me.

I'm alone on the white-blanketed platform whose tiny roof offers little protection from the driving snow. As I turn my overcoat right side up and slip it on, my pulse still racing from the excitement, I hope my frantic calculations were correct. I wonder if the next train really *will* come along and take me to Munich. . . .

Over time, the Abbey of Fulda became richer and richer, until by the thirteenth century it owned enough land to become a territorial state, and its abbot held the rank of a Prince of the Holy Roman Empire. By this time only noblemen could be admitted as monks, and Fulda, once famous for its scrupulous observance of monastic discipline, began to grow lax. The monks led a very comfortable existence, hardly appropriate for religious men whose founder once wrote that "a monk's life ought always to be a little Lent." They could no longer hear the call to holiness. Although in real need of renewal, the abbey went untouched by the great

monastic reforms happening elsewhere in Europe, and the monks continued their worldly ways for a few more decades. . . .

A fuzzy point of yellow light appears in the distance, getting larger
as it emerges out of the gray afternoon. The familiar throb of a diesel
locomotive mixes with the hiss of wind and snow as the Munich-bound
express rumbles in right on time. I climb aboard and I work my way
down the aisle. I slump into an empty seat, my heart still thumping from
my narrow escape.

The colorless scenery is sliding by the window again; my pulse starts to
slow down at last. I begin to realize what a close call I have just had: what
if I hadn't looked at that schedule when I did? What if I'd waited one more
minute before glancing at it? I had been sitting there quite at ease, with
all my things spread out for a long leisurely trip, when suddenly I had ten
seconds to scoop up all my belongings and beat an undignified retreat.

All Christians ought to treat life as a journey that may end at any
time. Monks especially are trained to live in such a way that they are
ready to leave at a moment's notice. It is dangerous for a monk—or for
any Christian—to begin to "settle-down," becoming attached to material
comforts or entangled in the quest for possessions, power, and prestige.

So what about me? Do I get so wrapped up in my everyday work or in
my worries that I no longer think much about God? Do I ever, like those
noblemen-monks of Fulda in the 1300s, get too distracted or too comfortable, and forget that I'm on a journey to somewhere else? Inevitably,
though, someday the Lord is going to say, "Wake up! This is Fulda, and
you've got to get off—right now!"

Outside the window night has fallen, and the frozen snowscape of
Hesse is rolling past unseen. As the train clacks its way south I pick up the
schedule from the seat beside me and double-check the arrival time for
Munich. Just making sure.

Reflection

During Lent we try to be more conscious than usual of being prepared for the Son of man to come "at an hour you do not expect" (Matt.
24:44, RSV). If someone were to look at the way you use creature comforts, food, or money, would they have the impression that you are on a
pilgrimage, and that your permanent home is in fact somewhere else? Or
would they conclude that this world is in fact your home, and that you
don't plan to move on?

Look at the various things you're attached to. Is there something which you
can do without during Lent just to remind yourself that you're on a journey?

Sacred Scripture (Heb. 13:14, RSV)

"For here we have no lasting city, but we seek the city which is to come."

Rule of Benedict
(Chapter 4, "The Tools for Good Works," vv. 46–47)

"Yearn for everlasting life with holy desire. Day by day remind yourself that you are going to die."

Saturday of the
Second Week of Lent

Saint Etienne du Mont, Paris:
Persevering

Glowing high overhead is the gray dome of the Panthéon, that pompous monument to France's military glory. My morning walk is taking me through the hilly Parisian neighborhood of *le quartier de la montagne de Sainte Geneviève*, "Saint Genevieve's Mountain." It's named after the city's patroness, who saved Paris from destruction by the Huns in the fifth century. The Panthéon is built on the site of a church dedicated to

Paris – St Eustack   10

Genevieve, and the plaza behind it still bears her name. I continue two blocks farther up the hill to visit the church that contains the relics of—who else?—Saint Genevieve.

Saint Etienne du Mont was built in 1492 to serve the workers employed by a nearby Benedictine abbey, and has undergone several transformations since then. In fact, this morning another restoration project blocks the main portals with sheets of bare plywood, so I have to find my way in through a side door.

I step into a silent world that is awash in pale golden light. Gentle silver sunshine filters through the stained glass windows, making the gray walls glow with dappled blues and reds. The elegant vertical lines and the joyful airy lightness of the place bring a wide smile to my face. Stretching across the middle of the church is a delicate bridge of carved marble with a graceful spiral staircase at either end. I reach for my little guidebook and find that this is a *jube*, or rood screen, dating from the Renaissance; it's the only one left in Paris. I stand still and just watch its polished stone glisten in the quiet light. The next paragraph in the book notes that the round pillars are another inheritance from the Renaissance, while the pointed arches and stonework are pure Gothic.

In the space of just a few minutes, Saint Etienne has become one of my favorite churches in Paris.

I wander into the side chapel that contains the remains of Saint Genevieve. Inside this shadowy little space I have to tilt the guidebook page toward the meager light and squint: during the Revolution a mob broke into the church and emptied the saint's coffin into the Seine. Part of the casket and some of the relics were recovered, however, and were returned to her chapel, where they now lie undisturbed in a rich reliquary. I picture the angry mob storming into the church and laying angry hands on the precious relics of their patron saint.

I turn around to face a small altar. Its tabernacle is flanked by a pair of wooden statues, each about four feet high. My book says the one on the right, holding a white candle, is Saint Genevieve herself. In the dim shadows it takes a couple of moments before I notice that she is not alone. Perched on her left shoulder like some evil bird is a small, dark-brown demon. His brow knit in fierce concentration, and his cheeks puffed with foul breath, he is trying to blow out the flame of the white candle the saint is holding. The dark figure is comical, but also a little unnerving. Then I notice, on her other shoulder, a little white-robed angel calmly waiting, with a lighted taper in his hand. The plot is obvious: every time the evil spirit blows out Genevieve's candle, the good angel simply reaches over and lights it again.

I sit down on a wicker-seated chair facing the altar to rest and pray for a few moments. I start to meditate on this painted wooden statue and the little drama that has been unfolding on her shoulders for hundreds of years. Its charming, simple theology seems naive at first, but I've learned not to laugh too fast at the spiritual imagery of our ancestors in the faith.

The stories the desert mothers and fathers told about demons are often quite insightful and subtle. In their view the demonic stood not only for the evil forces that attack us from outside, but also for everything that is disordered and incomplete inside of us. "The demon of greed" they would say, "came to a brother one day. . . ." or, "The demon of pride approached a brother in his cell. . . ." Maybe this statue was the local Benedictines' homage to the wisdom of their ancient forbears of the Egyptian desert.

As I look at the nasty little demon with the puffed cheeks, I remember what our senior monk, Father Celestine, used to say all the time: "The Devil is always stirring things up!" The master of dissension and discord likes to sneak in and disrupt any good thing he sees happening. He may try to blow out your candle by overwhelming you with distractions when you're trying to pray, or by showering you with feelings of frustration and resentment when you're trying to be kind to some difficult person.

Ancient monastic tradition taught that another favorite weapon of the evil one is discouragement. He just keeps coming and coming after you, trying to wear you down. He blows out the feeble flame of hope in your heart, but God's angel re-lights it. The devil blows it out again, and the angel lights it once more. The demon keeps repeating the pattern over and over, hoping that one day you'll grow weary of the battle and throw up your hands in despair.

This statue sends a beautiful message to people who feel discouraged: although life may indeed be a struggle at times, there's no reason to lose heart. When the flame of patience gets blown out in some frustrating situation, or when the last flicker of brotherly love dies because of something someone does to me, I can remember this statue of Saint Genevieve: God's angel is always there to re-light my candle. No matter how many times my own shortcomings and vices may extinguish the flame, the Lord always lets me start over. I may get tired of the battle, but God's angel with the lighted taper never does. Let the devil whisper words of discouragement, and try to make me grow weary of constantly repeating the same old mistakes and sins. Let him tell me that God is tired of my obvious inability to keep my candle burning. The patient angel with the taper will always be there to rekindle the flame one more time.

I stand up to continue my tour of Saint Etienne du Mont. First, though, I step over to the bank of votive lights flickering serenely in the shadows near Genevieve's statue. After dropping ten francs into the slot, I reach out with a little taper and light a big white candle.

Reflection

Think of some prolonged struggle you are going through, or which you may have gone through in the past, one which got pretty discouraging. How did the Lord keep rekindling the flame in you? Was it some particular person, some thought, some event?

Prayer, *lectio*, and acts of charity can be effective ways of overcoming discouragement. Ask the Lord to keep renewing your sense of hope and perseverance not just on the Lenten journey, but all along life's pilgrim road.

Sacred Scripture (Ps. 27:1–3, RSV)

The LORD is my light and my salvation; whom shall I fear?
The LORD is the stronghold of my life; of whom shall I be afraid?
When evildoers assail me, uttering slanders against me,
my adversaries and foes, they shall stumble and fall.
Though a host encamp against me, my heart shall not fear;
though war arise against me, yet I will be confident.

Rule of Benedict
(Chapter 4, "The Tools for Good Works," v. 74)

"And finally, never lose hope in God's mercy."

THE THIRD WEEK OF LENT

The Call to Conversion

For forty years Yahweh kept calling the Israelites deeper into the wilderness, and leading them farther along the road to conversion by teaching them lessons in trust, faithfulness, and love of God and of one another. After concentrating during the first two and a half weeks of Lent on our brokenness and our need to battle against temptation, we now turn to a more positive side of the Lenten observance: answering God's call to conversion by cultivating a life of virtue.

The same Lord who called the Hebrews to conversion calls you and me as well, especially during the desert days of Lent. Each of the six meditations this week deals with a virtue that is part of the conversion experience. Each of them is also specifically encouraged by Benedict in the *Rule*: listening in "Aubrac," good example in "Esteville," moderation and balance in "Dieppe," singleness of heart in "Padua," forgiveness in "Piray River," and openness to others in "Ciudad del Este."

Monday of the Third Week of Lent

Aubrac, France:
Listening

My feet are sore. I've been following the red-and-white trail markers for several hilly miles. They have led me along muddy cow paths, beside rough stone walls and barbed-wire fences, through thick woods, and across lush meadows in the rugged uplands of central France. I'm alone except for an occasional fellow-hiker, and a few friendly cows who ignore me as I tiptoe uneasily in their pasture within a few feet of them. The hiking trail, officially called "GR-65," follows a path worn by thousands of medieval pilgrims. They were walking the 800 miles from Le Puy in France to Santiago de Compostela in northwestern Spain to venerate the relics of Saint James the Apostle. Under a bleak, threatening sky, I'm making my own pilgrim way to the town of Aubrac with my mind on those hearty predecessors who trudged hundreds of dangerous, weary miles to fulfill their pilgrimage vows.

AUBRAC

At last, from the top of a grassy hill, I spot a lazy little village loafing in a patch of sunlight a couple of miles ahead. That must be Aubrac: a cluster of gray granite buildings and a few tall green trees. It looks out of place, as if some careless giant has dropped it by mistake into the middle of the rolling meadows.

I flop down in the soft, fragrant grass beside the path to rest my feet and to make a quick sketch of the tiny town. Its monastery and surrounding wall are gone, as are most of the other original buildings. Only a couple of sturdy, stone two-story inns, a low Romanesque church, and the Tower of the English remain.

Behind me I can hear the ghostly footfalls of pious phantom travelers on their way to and from Compostela, and I no longer feel alone.

When my sketch is finished, I stand up, dust myself off, shoulder my knapsack, and pick up the trail again as it winds its way down the sloping meadows toward Aubrac. The church steeple disappears behind a hill and pops up once more a few minutes later. Then it hides a second time, only to reappear in a couple of moments. My feet start to ache again. To take my mind off the soreness, I try to remember what I've read about Aubrac.

In the 1200s, a Flemish knight was making the difficult pilgrimage from Le Puy westward toward Compostela. Early on he had to cross these wild Aubrac highlands. He was waylaid by robbers on his outward journey across the uninhabited uplands. Then, on his return trip, he was suddenly engulfed in a freak blizzard near the same place. The knight made a vow that if he arrived home safely from his perilous trip he would have a way station built halfway across the Aubrac wilderness to help the pilgrims who were to come after him. The present hamlet of Aubrac proves that he was a man of his word. The order of Knights Hospitallers founded a priory here that would grow to be a sizable cluster of about a dozen buildings. While some of these religious men were offering lodging and food to the travelers, others, knights on horseback, would ride through the countryside hunting down robbers.

The squat church steeple pops into view again. That must be the home of Maria.

Her full name is *Maria, la Cloche des Perdus*, "Maria, the Lost People's Bell." Every evening around sundown the bell was tolled for two hours to guide any wayfarers who might still be out on the pilgrim trail, caught by the sudden onset of darkness. Whenever there was a heavy fog or a bad storm that made traveling more dangerous than usual, Maria sang out at regular intervals to act as a sort of homing device for unfortunate travelers wandering out on the uplands. Anyone lost in the wilderness could just listen for the bell and then follow the sound to the safety of the town.

Most of us have times when we feel bewildered or overwhelmed by relentless demands of family, job, and so on. The pilgrim travelers crossing the hazardous uplands of Aubrac have a lesson for us at such moments: they realized the value of listening. They knew that to find their way through the fog or the dark, they needed to listen for that bell. It was especially hard to hear Maria above the roar of wind and rain, so the trick was to stand still, be quiet, and listen very hard. After a while, they would begin to catch faint whispers of her voice riding on the wind, and that would be enough to guide them in the right direction through the storm.

If the gospel life is a constant response to Christ's call, then it makes sense that listening for that call should be an essential part of our life. The very first word of Benedict's *Rule* is "Listen!" And in that *Rule* he offers some help for listening that may be of use to any Christian. First, monastic and indeed all of Christian spiritual tradition teaches the need for frequent quiet prayer, for "resting in God." If our life is to have any real meaning, we have to be connected with the world of silence where God dwells, deep down in our innermost selves. In the expectant quiet of prayer and meditation the voice of the Spirit of truth speaks to us. Of course, silence can be scary. It's even scarier when the voice that speaks out of the quiet tells us something we don't want to hear, such as a truth about ourselves that we're unwilling to deal with. Maybe the bell will tell us we're heading off in the wrong direction and then we'll have to stop and change our life's direction. No wonder so many people try to fill every moment with noise—they're afraid that they might hear the sound of the bell calling them to turn around.

A second help for listening is Benedict's advice that we "listen with the ear of our heart" to what the Spirit has to say. For most of us, our workday is filled with a loud roar of activity—earning a living, caring for our children, working on our marriage, paying our bills. We can learn, however, how to listen with the ear of our heart to the events around us, and hear in them the guiding sound of the bell. A coworker marches toward me with a telltale look in her eye, and I steel myself. She's probably going to try to blame me for that fiasco at the meeting this morning. Well, just let her try. She'll get an earful. Then the woman walks past; she wasn't coming to see me at all! But I was ready to be ugly with her. That's the sound of the distant bell telling me that I'm getting off the path.

A teenage son comes up to his mother and spontaneously offers, "I'll be happy to babysit for a while if you need to go grocery shopping." Shocked, she begins to pray: "Sometimes, Jesus, just when I think I've been a total failure with that kid, he does something like this. Thank you for the encouragement! You must have known I needed it." The ear of her heart has heard the sound of the bell over the shouts from the playroom and the rock music on the radio upstairs, assuring her that she is on the right path.

The trail has now joined a paved road. As I approach the village, I can make out the mustard-colored moss on the church wall and a red bicycle leaning against the side of a house. I can almost feel the presence of the Hospitallers who once made this a welcome haven for weary pilgrims. Everything is perfectly still; the ear of my heart can hear Maria ringing from her tower.

I walk past the Tower of the English and the little church with its bell tower. I notice an old stone inn farther down the road on the right. The friendly smoke curling from its chimney draws me, hungry and thirsty, to its door. Aubrac at last—and my feet have stopped hurting.

Reflection

What are God's favorite ways of speaking to you? What changes might you make in your life to make it easier for the ear of your heart to hear God speaking?

A worthwhile Lenten exercise is to try to identify some of the emotional and moral "noise" in your life. Another is to lower the level of physical noise around you by limiting your use of television, radio, and so forth. These practices are not ends in themselves, but they can help us to hear better what God is telling us during this season.

Sacred Scripture (Jer. 7:23)

"Obey my voice, and I will be your God, and you shall be my people; and walk only in the way I command you."

Rule of Benedict (Prologue, vv. 9–10)

"Let us open our eyes to the light that comes from God, and our ears to the voice from heaven that every days calls out this charge: If you hear his voice today, do not harden your hearts."

Tuesday of the
Third Week of Lent

Esteville, France:
Living Example

My friend Bernard and his wife, Colette, and I are heading across the flat green farmland of Normandy toward an obscure village by the name of Esteville. Little pointed church steeples play hide-and-seek behind the distant rows of trees as we drive.

We are about to drop in unannounced on one of the best known and most venerated people in all of France, l'Abbé Pierre. Although this Catholic priest is famous in France and Europe, he's practically unknown in America, so Bernard has to spend the time filling me in as he drives.

In the early 1950s, Father Pierre Groués, a young diocesan priest, opened his house to several homeless men. He called his group the "Emmaus Community." In order to support themselves, they began picking over Paris's city dumps and selling what they found to junk dealers. They used their surplus income to buy large vacant lots and build simple houses on them for families of the working poor.

In January of 1954, Abbé Pierre was deeply touched by the plight of the homeless men and women he saw sleeping on the sidewalks of Paris in the sub-freezing cold. When he realized that no one was doing anything for these people, he, poor as he himself was, began driving into Paris every night with food for the cold and hungry and forgotten. As the weeks of unusual cold continued, he put up huge tents in vacant lots in the center of Paris to serve as shelters.

We're passing through a farming village. The sturdy silent farm folk look like characters from Guy de Maupassant's short stories. A road sign points to the town of Totes—this is the land of Madame Bovary.

In that same January of 1954, a woman froze to death on a Paris sidewalk, still clutching in her hand the eviction notice that had put her out of her little apartment and into the winter night to die. When Abbé Pierre told this story in church the next morning, the parishioners insisted that the rest of the country needed to hear about the horrible plight of France's homeless. So he prepared an address for broadcast on the radio and, with his incredible powers of persuasion, actually got a courageous radio official to preempt regular programming and allow him to deliver his plea. Up until that time, Abbé Pierre and his Emmaus brothers had been almost alone in the fight to help the homeless. This obscure priest had been living with the poor, encouraging them, bringing them a sense of dignity and of being loved, and had been building houses for homeless families.

That night on the radio, his straightforward statement of the problem and his impassioned appeal for everyone's immediate help pricked France's conscience. Some say it actually gave France back her soul. The plea, broadcast nationally, caused an immediate outpouring of good will from old and young, rich and poor, in every part of the country, but especially in Paris. As an afterthought, the young priest added a request to Parisians to bring their gifts and their help to a certain hotel just off the Champs Elysées. Within half an hour there was a traffic jam for blocks on every side of the hotel, as good-hearted Parisians brought hundreds of warm coats, sweaters, and blankets, and thousands of francs in cash.

Abbé Pierre started delivering more radio addresses and talks that roused the nation's sense of social responsibility and, in fact, changed France's attitude toward the problems of the poor and the homeless. Over the next forty years, he would become the voice of the voiceless in France, acting as the country's conscience in debates on social legislation. To this day, polls show that Frenchmen still consider him the most trustworthy public figure in the nation. This is the man I'm about to meet.

Bernard pulls to the side of the road and stops to consult the map. Ulysse, the family poodle, sticks his nose into the map, too, and, tilting his head to one side, seems to study the route carefully. The car windows remain closed against the brisk autumn air. Through them, I see a couple of rugged stone farmhouses squatting nearby.

Although retired now because of age and failing health, Abbé Pierre has hardly been silent. In fact, a few weeks ago in the midst of the French presidential campaign and the debate over the economic implications of the new European Economic Union he posed a question to France's conscience. "*Et les autres?*" he asked publicly—"And what about the others?" Once again, the Abbé was speaking up on behalf of the poor and the forgotten.

We drive a few kilometers farther and then stop to ask a young woman for Abbé Pierre's house. She points us to a nondescript, rambling collection of old brick farm buildings loafing, as if tired, beside the road. A tiny hand-painted "Emmaus" sign marks the driveway. As we pull into the bumpy parking area in back, I decide that the simple place seems just right for Abbé Pierre and his ragpickers.

The next thing I know, I'm standing in an enclosed courtyard shaking hands with a pleasant old man with a white beard and a navy blue beret. Abbé Pierre's slow gait hardly matches his bright, alert eyes and his quick, kindly smile.

Bernard, who is also meeting him for the first time, introduces himself and his wife. He then presents me as an American Benedictine whose monastery in the center of Newark, New Jersey, runs a school that welcomes poor children. The old priest nods in understanding and asks if I know a certain friend of his who works with the homeless in Harlem. We chat easily for a minute or two. Instead of radiating a sense of energy or strength Abbé Pierre is surrounded by an aura of serenity—he is a man at peace with himself.

Then, not wanting to wear out our welcome, I kneel down and ask him for his blessing. After he finishes blessing me and I've stood up again, he quietly asks me, "And now, Father, your blessing, please."

A moment later we're back in the car driving away. Bernard is so overwhelmed he can't even speak, so we just ride in silence for some time, thinking about what we've just experienced.

I start to ask myself, what is the secret of this little man's great success? Part of it, certainly, is his effective use of mass media and his flair for the dramatic word or gesture. But lots of people have that. There must be something else. I think of a recent political cartoon in a French newspaper that concerned Abbé Pierre's forcing the French presidential candidates to take a stand on such social issues as poverty and low-cost housing: it shows the two major candidates wearing false beards and berets, each masquerading as Abbé Pierre, while the real Abbé looks on. The caption says simply "Beware of imitations!" This suggests the most important reason for his success: Abbé Pierre is clearly the real thing. He opened his house to homeless derelicts and misfits, gathering them into a community where they could find love and self-respect. He then set them to work putting up rudimentary housing for working people who couldn't afford a place to live. So when, in the winter of 1954, he spoke up spontaneously and sincerely on behalf of the homeless, his voice had a compelling ring of truth and authority about it because he had been living with the poor and devoting his whole life to them.

And now, his fifty years of living and working with the indigent have given him a license to speak up whenever the state or its citizens start forgetting their duty toward the homeless. And people pay attention. Abbé

Pierre has moral authority—a priceless thing for anyone who wants to preach the gospel. It doesn't seem all that complicated: he simply lives what he teaches. By being an actual flesh and blood example of Christ's love for the poor, he challenges a whole nation of Christians to live out their own call to gospel holiness and justice.

As we drive back through the lush green countryside, I wonder about myself: how much moral authority do I have when I call others to respond to the gospel? Does my way of treating my students give me the authority to challenge them to lives of selfless love? Does my way of responding to my brother monks give a ring of truth to my sermons at our community Mass when I summon them to endless, Christ-like patience?

Abbé Pierre has just given me more than his blessing, he's given me a challenge: to make my preaching of the gospel believable by living it better myself.

Reflection

Conversion includes being a good example to others, including people we don't even know are watching us. In what circumstances might the Lord be counting on you to teach others by your good example? How might you improve in this regard?

Think of some relationships where you need to have moral authority (e.g. as a parent, a boss, or an advisor). Is there one of these where your moral authority could be strengthened if you improved your own behavior?

Sacred Scripture (Matt. 23:1–3, RSV)

"Then said Jesus to the crowds and to his disciples, 'The scribes and the Pharisees sit on Moses' seat; so practice and observe whatever they tell you, but not what they do; for they preach, but do not practice.'"

Rule of Benedict
(Chapter 2, "Qualities of the Abbot," v. 12)

"[The abbot] must point out to them all that is good and holy more by example than by words."

Wednesday of the
Third Week of Lent

Dieppe, France:
Balancing

Sitting as she does at the water's edge on the rugged Normandy coastline, Dieppe is constantly having her hair blown back by the winds that whip across the English Channel. From my cliff-top vantage point I can see that her streets are laid out and the gates in her old town walls placed in such a way as to reduce the effect of the constant sea breeze. At my feet, halfway down the cliff, a charming little castle, perched solidly atop a rocky knob, looks out across the Channel.

Dieppe
Le Château

In the center of the scene a great grassy esplanade runs right along the water's edge, separating the front row of the town's buildings on the right from the beach on the left. Ancient engravings show that this same broad field, several blocks long and a hundred yards wide, has changed very little over the passing centuries. Despite the low clouds heavy with threatening rain, the green meadow is especially crowded today. Tugging impatiently against their invisible strings, dozens of bright-colored kites are riding the steady wind. The stiff breeze holds them motionless, their tails pointing straight inland toward the roofs and steeples of town. There are box kites of red and white, cylinder kites of yellow and orange, a green kite that looks like a quilted saltine, and a couple that seem like big blue rubber rafts floating on an unseen sea.

The perpetual breeze makes the beachfront park a favorite spot for kite-fliers all year round, and this week Dieppe is the proud host of an international kite-fliers' convention. Her streets teem with folks from Asia, the Americas, Africa, Australia, and Europe who share a passion for building and flying kites, and her skies are alive with their colorful creations. I have the good luck to get invited to the official reception for the participants at the *hôtel de ville*, Dieppe's modern town hall. The speeches include many references to the beautiful harmony of nations among the participants engaged in such an innocent, childlike exercise of the spirit. While the various foreign delegations are presenting their symbolic gifts to the mayor, a question keeps pushing to the front of my mind: are these people serious? On the one hand, they are clearly in earnest, because this kind of kiting involves a real commitment of time, money, and energy. On the other hand, these grown men and women spend hours standing in fields holding strings and watching their pretty-colored playthings slide and glide in the breeze.

As the ceremony continues, I realize that kite-flying is neither serious nor playful; it's . . . *spoudogeloios!*

I came across this tongue-twisting adjective from classical Greek many years ago, and we've been fast friends ever since. It's a combination of two words: *spoudos*, "serious, earnest," and *gelein*, "to laugh." So *spoudogeloios* means something like "grave-merry" or "serious-playful." For the ancient Greeks, the ideal person is one who is poised between the earnest and the playful, who travels through life with the evenness of spirit that comes from balancing heaviness and lightness. If you are *spoudogeloios*, you don't take yourself too seriously, yet you appreciate the deep and eternal dimension of the human situation and strive to live accordingly.

It seems to me that this is a marvelous description of Christian holiness: the saint is one who manages to keep the serious and the playful in balance.

There is a light side to Christianity. The very word "gospel" means "good news"; the victory has already been won. "If God is for us, who can be against us?" "I am with you always; yes, to the end of time." "You have turned my mourning into dancing." Saint Irenaeus once spoke of the spiritual life as "a divine children's game."

However, our life of faith has a "heavy" side as well. The Scriptures are equally full of grave passages: "Keep sober and alert, because your enemy the devil is on the prowl...." "Go away from me, with your curse upon you, to the eternal fire . . . for I was hungry and you never gave me food. . . ." "For it is not against human enemies that we have to struggle, but against . . . the spirits of evil in the heavens."

A Christian needs to balance the heavy and the light, like a kite that feels both the string tugging it to earth and the wind lifting it off toward the stars. Some of us, though, are so grim about our relationship with God that our religion becomes a deadly serious, white-knuckled, and humorless project, centered on sin and eternal damnation. Such "heavy" believers just can't lighten up; their kites are too heavy to fly.

Others, however, are too casual about their life in the Spirit. They want a God who is like a kindly, generous old uncle who makes no real demands on them. These believers avoid any talk of sin, self-discipline, or the need to deal with the potentially destructive forces at work in the inner self. Their kites are not anchored in the sober truth of the gospel and its demands for constant conversion, but go flying away on the breeze, completely out of touch with reality.

Balancing the serious and the playful, the light and the heavy, is a skill that comes only with long practice. It takes time to arrive at wisdom, to become *spoudogeloios*. This is why, in the monastery or anywhere else, it is the elders, who have been at it for a long while, who usually give the best example of balance. They've learned the hard way how to avoid the extremes of heaviness and lightness, and live suspended serenely between heaven and earth.

The ceremony ends with a typical French offering of champagne and hors d'oeuvres. As I elbow my way among the Japanese, the Australians, and the Samoans, all talking (I presume) about their kites, I try not to spill my champagne. I ask the Lord to give me a little of the delightful balance I see among these playful-serious people. Or, even better, the gracefulness of a colorful kite as it floats easily in the happy tension between the unseen string and the invisible wind.

Reflection

Lent is a time to look at some of the forces in your life that may need to be kept in better balance: controlling versus letting go, busyness versus leisure, tension versus relaxation, severity versus gentleness. Choose one pair that seems most in need of attention. How can Lent help you to find a healthier balance? Make a decision to address the problem.

Is your approach to the keeping of Lent balanced between heavy and light? If not, how might you correct the imbalance?

Sacred Scripture (Prov. 2:1, 2, 9–12a, RSV)

My son, if you receive my words and treasure up my commandments with you, making your ear attentive to wisdom and inclining your heart to understanding; . . . Then you will understand righteousness and justice and equity, every good path; for wisdom will come into your heart, and knowledge will be pleasant to your soul; discretion will watch over you; understanding will guard you; delivering you from the way of evil.

Wisdom of the Desert

Abbot Mark once said to Abbot Arsenius: "It is good, is it not, to have nothing in your cell that just gives you pleasure? For example, once I knew a brother who had a little wildflower that came up in his cell, and he pulled it out by the roots." "Well," said Abbot Arsenius, "that is all right. But each one should act according to his own spiritual way. And if one were not able to get along without the flower, he should plant it again."[3]

---

3. Thomas Merton, trans., *The Wisdom of the Desert: Sayings from the Desert Fathers of the Fourth Century* (New York: New Direction Books, 1970), 67–68.

Thursday of the Third Week of Lent

Padua, Italy:
Leading One Life

I'm on a walking tour of Padua, following the free map provided by the Tourist Office. I started at the railroad station (the first stop on the map) and have been following the red line painted on the sidewalk. It has already led past ancient Roman walls, down busy streets and across wide piazzas, passing the great brown basilica of "*Il Santo*," Saint Anthony of Padua, wonder-worker and finder of lost articles, and has started to circle back after reaching the Benedictine monastery with its immense church dedicated to Santa Giustina, the patron saint of the city.

My own patron saint, Albert the Great, was a Dominican scholar. His tremendous breadth of knowledge in physical sciences, philosophy, and theology earned him the title of *Doctor Universalis*, "Universal Doctor." I have walked in his footsteps a couple of times already in my European travels. In Paris, I strolled down the quiet street named after him: rue du Maître Albert, "Master Albert Street," on the Left Bank. It was near there that he studied and taught from 1241 to 1248. In Cologne, I stayed for a few days with the Dominican Friars at Sankt Andreas Kirche, the lovely Romanesque church where Albert's body lies in a plain stone sarcophagus in the crypt. On today's day-trip from Venice, I hope to meet up with the great Doctor of the Church once again, this time at the University of Padua.

The university is a large blue "56" printed over a busy shopping street near the center of my map. I follow the red line toward the spot, watching for my patron's footprints.

The official date of the founding of the great school is 1222. The very next summer, Jordan of Saxony, the successor of Saint Dominic as master general of the Dominicans, came to Padua in hopes of attracting candidates to the new Order of Preachers. Among his ten recruits, he wrote, were "two sons of two great German lords, one . . . has resigned rich benefices and is truly noble in mind and body." Tradition has it that the second young man was the future Albertus Magnus, Saint Albert the Great.

For its first three hundred years, the university didn't even have its own buildings, so I'm not likely to find any places where young Albert actually studied. What I do find this afternoon are plenty of worn-out four-story buildings with modern shops on the street level. I cross avenues filled with noisy noonday traffic and stroll along crowded sidewalks. The red line takes me past computer stores, leather boutiques, trattorias, florists, and booksellers to the spot shown on my map. But I still don't see any university. There is, however, a marker that brags that Professor Galileo Galilei perfected the telescope while teaching here between 1592 and 1608.

I remember being fascinated as a college student by the life of a philosopher who taught in the University of Padua at about the same time as Galileo. He had the unforgettable name of Professor Pietro Pomponazzi. What was even more impressive than his name was his double life. A devout, practicing Catholic, he would go to church and worship God, then walk to the university and teach his students that the truths of philosophy and logic completely contradict those of faith. He taught that according to philosophy the soul cannot be immortal, but that according to theology it is. He saw no problem in holding both teachings as true.

My philosophical musings are rudely interrupted by the screech of brakes and the ill-tempered blast of a horn. I've just stepped off the curb and am blinking stupidly at the red Ferrari that has almost hit me. The driver screams at me in loud Italian and roars off flourishing some quaint hand gesture that undoubtedly dates back to the days of the obscene Emperor Caligula.

Professor Pomponazzi led two separate lives. First, he was a loyal Catholic, holding to the beliefs and practices of the Church. Second, he was a philosopher, following the strict demands of reason and the laws of evidence, the conclusions of which were often at odds with the teachings of his faith. He somehow managed to hold that both contradictory sets of beliefs were true—he simply kept them entirely separated from one another in his mind.

It's interesting that the Oration for the Mass on the feast of Albert the Great notes that the saint was known for his "talent of combining human wisdom and divine faith." Unlike Pomponazzi, Albert did not lead two lives. He saw everything he did, whether in biology, chemistry, or philosophy, as somehow infused with the holy, with the presence of God.

Finding no trace of anything that looks like a school building, I take it on faith that I'm standing right in the middle of the famous university where Albert studied and Pietro Pomponazzi taught. I decide to keep following the faithful red line back to the railroad station.

In a slightly different way from my professor friend, many modern Christians see themselves as leading two lives. First, there is the life that has to do with God, angels, heaven, and hell. This is called "religion." At most, it demands an hour on Sunday, the avoidance of gross sins, and intellectual agreement with a set of doctrines. Second, and far more important, there is the life that deals with everyday concerns such as earning a living, making the car payments, changing diapers, and keeping the house clean. This is called "real life." Since many Christians can see little or no connection between their religious beliefs and the practicalities of their "real" life, they lead two distinct lives that at times are even opposed to each other.

Saint Benedict sees no opposition between the "holy" and the "earthly." The abbot, for example, who is the spiritual head and teacher of the monastery, also has the down-to-earth tasks of making sure the bell gets rung on time, assigning the daily work to the brethren, and keeping an inventory of the monastery's tools and clothing. The "cellarer," on the other hand, who has the very practical charge of distributing to the monks all the various material necessities, is to do so with the same compassion and concern for everyone's spiritual well-being as the abbot: he should be "like a father to the whole community." "If any brother happens to make an unreasonable demand of him, he should not reject him with disdain and cause him distress, but reasonably and humbly deny the improper request." This monk who is in charge of the store room "must show every care and concern for the sick, children, guests, and the poor, knowing for certain that he will be held accountable for all of them on the day of judgment." So, is his a secular job or a spiritual one?

Saint Albert had the same insight that Benedict had: it is in such so-called "secular" things that we are most likely to meet God. A young mother's spirituality revolves around feeding and caring for her child. A middle-aged man who is considering changing careers suddenly learns what it means to trust in God's goodness. His insecure job situation certainly involves weighing such factors as salary and job satisfaction, but it is also the place where he is going to meet—right now—the God who loves him and watches over him.

Every Christian is called to experience God's unconditional love working itself out in everyday events. For the young mother, for the fellow afraid of changing careers, for all of us, it's never a question of "prayer life" versus "real life." Saints don't lead two lives, but one. It is in our everyday experiences that we learn to grow in trust, to risk loving others, and to be compassionate to people in need. We can accept these opportunities or not, but we cannot say that they have nothing to do with our spiritual life.

The train station looms up ahead. The red line has brought me back to my starting point after a pleasant day in the company of an unlikely group: Saint Anthony and his lost articles, Galileo and his telescope, Albert the Great and his books, and Pietro Pomponazzi, the man who led two lives.

Reflection

Lent makes us aware of our faults and our need for penance, but it also helps us to see that God is already present to help and save us. So, it would be appropriate during this season to make a list of places or activities in your life where you might not usually think of encountering God. Then reflect on each place or activity individually and ask the Lord to show you how the Divine is present for you even there. Think of practical things that might help you to be aware of God's presence in the kitchen, in the car, or at the office.

Sacred Scripture (Rom. 10:6–8, RSV)

"But the righteousness based on faith says, Do not say in your heart, 'Who will ascend into heaven?' (that is, to bring Christ down) or 'Who will descend into the abyss?' (that is, to bring Christ up from the dead). But what does it say? The word is near you, on your lips and in your heart."

Rule of Benedict
(Chapter 31, "Qualifications of the Monastery Cellerar," vv. 6–9)

[The monastery cellerar] should not annoy the brothers. If any brother happens to make an unreasonable demand of him, he should not reject him with disdain and cause him distress, but reasonably and humbly deny the improper request. . . . He must show every care and concern for the sick, children, guests and the poor, knowing for certain that he will be held accountable for all of them on the day of judgment.

Friday of the
Third Week of Lent

Piray River, Bolivia:
Forgiving

"Are you waiting for a lift across the river?" asks Father Roger in his British-flavored Spanish.

"*¡Ah, si, Padre! ¡Gracias!*" the young man answers as he steps toward the rear door of our four-wheel-drive. I suppose that he's been sitting beside the two-rut track here for a couple of hours.

I'm riding in the front seat next to Father Roger, looking ahead through the dusty windshield at the boiling brown froth of the river that lies between us and the low greenery on the other bank. Several broad sand bars split the Piray into a dozen wide channels of unknown depth. We're on our way to a village outside of Santa Cruz in central Bolivia to see the newly reconditioned church that dates back to the time of the first Jesuit missionaries. Once you leave the main highway, there's no paved road to this village. What's worse, it's on the other side of the river—and there's no bridge.

During the past few weeks in the rectory of the English-speaking missionary priests of the Saint James Society, I've heard a few casual stories of one or another driver starting to ford some angry river and then getting carried off by the current. One such mishap had befallen a missionary not too long ago as he, his vehicle, and his passengers got washed down river. "He was okay, though. Wound up on a sandbar twenty yards downstream. I had to go out in the four-wheel-drive with the winch on front and pull him out," the narrator had said over dessert. River crossings attempted during very high water can end much more tragically, though. Everything depends on how high the river is.

Our young passenger perches on one of the two bench-seats that face each other just behind me, and the padre shifts into first gear. With visions of river water sloshing in onto my ankles I lift my knapsack off the floor, trying to be casual about it. I sneak a glance between my feet to check for articles that may float away when the water starts spurting through the doors.

"Well, here we go!" our driver announces cheerfully, as we lurch down the muddy track that gives way to the sandy slope of the riverbank. The first of the swift, coffee-colored strips of river lies right in front of us, and we plunge straight into it, in what seems to me a great act of faith. I ask myself, "How does he know that this channel won't turn out to be six feet deep?"

Now we're completely surrounded by the muddy water, rocking along up to our nonexistent hubcaps at a pretty good clip. Once I get used to it, it's sort of thrilling—just like in those articles I used to read as a kid in Maryknoll Missions Magazine. I look out my side window and watch the foamy water sliding by. As I stare down into the ripples beside me, I'm hypnotized, and all sense of time and distance disappears.

". . . he had been a missionary down here for several years by that time." Father Roger, almost shouting to be heard over the rumble of the engine, has begun a story. I've missed some of it already. He continues, "The river had been rising for several days, and the padre figured he'd never be able to drive across. It was 'first penance' day for the children in the mission church out here, and the catechists had the kids all excited about making their first confession. So he decides to drive out on the slim chance that he'll find the river passable. He turns off the highway and comes down the same road we just did. He meets a fellow along the way who gives him the bad news—no chance of driving across that afternoon. The kids will just have to wait for another day. . . ."

Whoosh! The wheels on the left side slump into a shallow dip in the river bed and my stomach jumps. Father Roger doesn't seem to notice, though, and goes right on with his tale as we crawl up onto a low sandbar and then plunge into the next channel.

"But the padre figures he's come this far so he may as well go on anyway and have a look at the river for himself. He continues on the road until he comes around that last bend right down by the river, where we just picked up our passenger. And guess what he sees there?"

Swoosh! We list sickeningly again, this time to my side. I stare wide-eyed at the bottom of the door, but all is still dry.

"Well, sure enough," continues the unperturbed Englishman behind the wheel, "the water was indeed very high—too high to drive through. But there, lined up along the road on his side of the river, were all the children, dressed up and waiting for their first confession! The parents had seen that the ford was too deep to drive across, but they didn't want their children to miss their first penance. So the fathers picked up their children and put them on their shoulders and carried them through the water to the priest's side of the river. And there they were, all ready for him when he got there. . . ."

Now we're slithering up the opposite bank, all four wheels churning in the loose sand until we're back onto the bumpy ruts of the mud track as it continues through the scruffy shrubbery and ragged trees. The relative safety of the jolting ride on solid ground soon lulls me into thinking about those fathers on that afternoon a few years ago. . . .

So many sincere parents give their families so much—in the way of material things. Those poor Bolivians couldn't give their children video games or electronic toys, dancing lessons or Little League baseball. Many probably couldn't offer them an education, or electricity in the house, or even decent drinking water. But they were able to give them the most meaningful gift a Christian parent can give a child—a God who loves us and forgives us. When the rising river threatened to keep the priest from getting to their church, the parents decided that if God couldn't get to their children, then they'd have to bring their children to God. So, hoisting their sons and daughters onto their shoulders, they set out. Across the ford they came that afternoon, laughing and shouting, wading through hip-high water, feeling for footholds, all the time carrying on their shoulders their little ones, bringing them to meet the God of forgiveness.

I wonder what those little Bolivian boys and girls learned about God that day when their fathers lifted them onto their shoulders and delivered them across the seething river? I know they learned something about being a Christian parent. . . .

A few houses start peeking out from behind the low trees now, then a wide clearing appears up ahead. . . .

By the end of life's journey, a Christian's shoulders ought to be aching with the effort of bringing others to meet the Lord through kind deeds, courageous example, and life-giving words of encouragement. More than once, I've had the experience of being lifted up and carried by someone right to the feet of the God of Mercy. On one occasion, I had to go to a brother and admit that a careless mistake of mine had just ruined the new electric typewriter I'd borrowed from him. His gentle response gave me an unforgettable lesson, a sense of what God's forgiveness must be like. Do I ever do that for people who come to me to apologize?

"That's it up ahead there, on the left!" Father Roger is pointing out the old Jesuit mission church. "That's the church those parents left behind when they took their kids across the Piray for first penance."

I hope that from now on, when I meet someone in need of forgiveness I'll remember the example of those determined fathers and mothers who hoisted their little ones on their shoulders and carried them across the river.

Reflection

Conversion means turning to God in a spirit of repentance for our sins. Think of one area where you particularly need God's forgiveness, and ask the Lord for pardon.

Is there one particular person who has taught you a lot about forgiveness? How often do you introduce others to the God of forgiveness by the forgiving them?

Sacred Scripture (John 8:3–11, RSV)

The scribes and the Pharisees brought a woman who had been caught in adultery, and placing her in the midst they said to him, "Teacher, this woman has been caught in the act of adultery. Now in the law Moses commanded us to stone such. What do you say about her?" . . . Jesus was left alone with the woman standing before him. Jesus looked up and said to her, "Woman, where are they? Has no one condemned you?" She said, "No one, Lord." And Jesus said, "Neither do I condemn you; go, and do not sin again."

Rule of Benedict
(Chapter 27, "The Abbot's Concern for the Excommunicated," vv. 8–9)

"[The Abbot] is to imitate the loving example of the Good Shepherd who left the ninety-nine sheep in the mountains and went in search of the one sheep that had strayed. So great was his compassion that he mercifully placed it on his sacred shoulders and so carried it back to the flock."

Saturday of the Third Week of Lent

Ciudad del Este, Paraguay: Being Open

The bus floats noisily on the sluggish stream of traffic and exhaust fumes. A few minutes after crossing the bridge from Brazil into Ciudad del Este, Paraguay, we come to a stop near the Paraguayan Immigration Office. My three fellow passengers and I get off the bus and meekly follow our driver into a dingy office where a uniformed man is slumped behind a cluttered desk. While his thick fingers crinkle the pages of my passport he slurs an incomprehensible question at me in Spanish. After months of traveling in foreign countries, I've found that the best solution to the problem of the incomprehensible question is simply to give an immediate and confident answer of some kind. So I nod and reply in Spanish that I've just visited the Iguazu Falls and am on my way back to Bolivia via Asunción, Paraguay. He likes this answer—I wonder what the question was?—and shoos me on my way with a friendly toss of my thoroughly thumbed passport.

We climb back on board and drive to the nearby bus terminal to pick up about twenty-five more passengers. Soon the almost-full bus finds the busy two-lane road that will take us all the way across Paraguay to Asunción. I settle into my seat next to a window for the five-hour ride.

In the past three days of visiting the breathtaking Cataracts of Iguazu, I've been in Argentina, Brazil, and Paraguay, bringing to fifteen the number of countries I've visited in my sabbatical travels. As comfortable as I am traveling in strange new places, wherever I go I'm always conscious of being an outsider, of being "different." People seem to be able to spot me from a mile away as a foreigner.

Once, for instance, after browsing for some minutes in a little souvenir shop in Brussels, I walked up to the counter and the saleswoman said, in English, "You are an American, of course." I exploded in fairly voluble French, "But I haven't said a word! How do you know I'm American, *madame*?" She couldn't explain it—she just knew, that's all.

And then there were those vendors selling little packets of sugar-coated peanuts in the parks of Paris. They prided themselves on spotting me at a hundred meters. As I approached one of those little carts its owner would ask smugly in bad English, "A beeg bahg or a leetle bahg, sir?" I always ignored him and answered in French, "*Un p'tit, s'il vous plaît!*" How did they know I'm an American? Was it the way I walk? Or maybe the way I wear my clothes?

A French woman who had studied for years in London and spoke fine British English heard me make an announcement at a multilingual Mass at Mont Saint Michel. She said to me afterward, "I love the way you pronounce English! I could listen to it all day! Say some sentences for me!" Even if Londoners might not share her gushing enthusiasm for my unmistakable American accent, people who hear me speaking English certainly can tell where I come from.

We're out of Ciudad del Este now. Along each side of the highway runs a wide swath that includes a dirt service road, strips of weeds, scraggly trees, and sometimes a bus stop shelter or a tumbledown snack bar. Along the outermost edge on either side widely varied buildings face toward the traffic. A flashy new Toyota salesroom sits uneasily beside a car repair shop of unpainted wood with a dirt floor.

Different nationality groups do have certain characteristics that are more or less typical. A particular Italian bus driver comes to mind. He pulled to a stop at this traffic light on the route into Florence. He looked both ways to make sure no cars were coming, then drove merrily through the red light and across the four-lane highway.

In Cologne, Germany, the pedestrians arranged themselves in a neat row on either side of me, their toes at the edge of the curb. The people facing us on the opposite side of the street did the same. We were waiting for the traffic light to change. No one moved until the signal said to walk. Don't even *think* about crossing against the light!

In Asunción, the capital of Paraguay, my stroll around downtown revealed only about four traffic lights. Drivers there just work things out among themselves without the help of red lights at intersections.

Traveling from one country to the next for some months has helped me to appreciate the remarkable variety that exists among various cultures and peoples.

We're now well out in the *campo*, the countryside. Cows and burros graze in the grass and gravel beside the road. Little children pad around in the red dust in front of pink or lavender one-room houses that face the highway in sets of four. Fountain-bursts of ragged palm leaves gush out of the ground without benefit of tree trunks. Slender pines make strange partners for the squat palms.

We seem to take on the characteristics of our homeland. I remember a phrase from a second-century biographer named Ennodius, who describes a local priest this way: "There was the outstanding priest, Bonosus, as celebrated for his holiness as for his noble bloodline, a Gaul by family origin but a native of heaven."

I gaze out of the smudged window at the volcano-shaped mounds of red earth beside the road—anthills as tall as a man—and I start to think. . . .

Actually, all of us are natives of heaven. Hmm. What would happen if I began to act like a native of heaven? I'd probably speak with a recognizable "foreign accent." People would know by my speech that I'm from somewhere else. The tones of kindness and patience in my voice would give my identity away. "Aha!" they'd say, "We know where *you're* from!"

Benedict tells his monks, "Your way of acting should be different from the world's way." But he continues in the same sentence, telling them exactly how they should be different from others: "the love of Christ must come before all else." If I carried myself the way Benedict suggests, with charity, trust, and humility, people would be able to recognize me as "an American by birth but a native of heaven." From a hundred yards away they could tell my real country of origin, or at least know that I'm "not from around here. . . ." In fact, the gospel calls every Christian to be that way. We're all natives of heaven, after all.

We crunch onto the dirt service road and pull to a stop in front of a Japanese pharmacy that sits beside the road next to a Japanese store-restaurant in the middle of nowhere. An Asian couple climbs aboard, and we roar off, leaving billows of dust and smoke.

The sun is sinking behind clumps of blue clouds that float on the watery orange sky. A young boy on horseback rides like a ghostly shadow among the slender trunks of tall palms, their shaggy heads silhouetted black against the sleepy sunset.

It's just about dark now in central Paraguay. Shouldn't I be feeling lonely or sad or at least ill at ease? After all, I am alone in a strange land, thousands of miles from home. But I don't feel like a foreigner this evening. No, right now I sense that I'm a fellow citizen of everyone on this bus. Our passports say we're from different countries, but we're all, like that saintly priest Bonosus, natives of heaven, and all on the road together, returning to our heavenly homeland.

I flick off the dim reading lamp and peer out into the darkness. On the horizon is the first faint glow of the lights of Asunción.

Reflection

The Lenten call to conversion challenges us to act according to our true identity—citizens of heaven. What is there about your way of living that would tell people that you're a citizen of heaven? On the other hand, are there perhaps some ways in which you've begun to act instead like the people around you who think that earth is all we get, and who are more interested in power and money?

Benedict insists that Lent be a community observance; in fact, he specifically forbids any monk to practice any kind of penance without the abbot's permission, so that the season can be observed by "the entire community." Lent, as he sees it, is not a time for retreating into a closed little world of God-and-me. Just the opposite: by calling us to works of charity, and by helping us to recognize our own sinfulness and our need for redemption, Lent reminds us of our common humanity with others.

Sacred Scripture (Phil. 3:18–20, NAB)

"For many, as I have often told you and now tell you even in tears, conduct themselves as enemies of the cross of Christ. Their end is destruction. Their God is their stomach; their glory is in their 'shame.' Their minds are occupied with earthly things. But our citizenship is in heaven, and from it we also await a savior, the Lord Jesus Christ."

Rule of Benedict (Chapter 72, "The Good Zeal of Monks," vv. 7–12)

"No one is to pursue what he judges better for himself, but instead, what he judges better for someone else. To their fellow monks they show the pure love of brothers; to God, loving fear; to their abbot, unfeigned and humble love. Let them prefer nothing whatever to Christ, and may he bring us all together to everlasting life."

THE FOURTH WEEK
OF LENT

Awareness of God's Presence

We saw in the first week that the wilderness was a place of trial and temptation for Israel. There was, however, a second and rather different tradition in the Old Testament, which thought of the wilderness experience as a unique time of intimacy with God, when Yahweh and the Chosen People came to know one another; it was a kind of honeymoon. This week the emphasis shifts to that second tradition, and celebrates the fact that God is always close to us on our journey.

The meditations for the Fourth Week, then, help us to be more aware of the varied ways in which our Savior walks with us every day. "Tuscany" celebrates Christ's presence in the people around us; "Gödöllő" suggests a way of looking for God; "Poitiers" and "Brussels" insist that God is a part of our lives even when we are unaware of the fact; "Saint Malo" looks at a normal response to discovering God in our world—thanksgiving; and "Assisi" reminds us of our duty to help others see God in the world.

Monday of the Fourth Week of Lent

Tuscany, Italy:
Recognizing Jesus

My head is full of images of gondolas and canals, arched bridges and flocks of pigeons. I've spent the last few days living with my brother Benedictines at the island abbey of San Giorgio in the middle of the bay of Venice. But now I'm on a train heading south to Tuscany. I changed trains a few minutes ago in Florence and am taking a half-hour ride out to the ancient monastery of Benedictine nuns in Pontassieve, where I'll be staying for the next four days.

Via Dai Neri - Florence

I glance out of the window and . . . wait a minute! I've never been anywhere near this part of Italy before, so why do I have the distinct feeling that I know this place? Those odd cypresses that look like great green feathers are familiar, for example. So is the little river that winds among castle-topped hills until it's lost in the distant blue-gray haze. Then I realize what's going on: I've been looking at these scenes my whole life in the backgrounds of famous paintings. Those great Florentine artists are so familiar that we call them by their first names—Michelangelo, Rafael, Leonardo. Their paintings are so much a part of our religious imagery that we take it for granted that Mary visited Elizabeth in an Italian villa with cypress trees in the background and that both women were dressed as Renaissance ladies. I look out the window again half expecting to see the Angel Gabriel suddenly appear on that marble terrace over there unrolling a long white banner, "*Ave, gratia plena!*" in front of a young Virgin. On the road in the distance I search for the exotic procession of camels carrying the three wise men and their gifts to a chubby Florentine bambino lying in the courtyard of that big farmhouse near the tracks.

The little train rattles along hillsides that are covered with vineyards and topped with towers, and follows the banks of the Arno past fallow fields, exhausted little garden plots, and genteelly decaying farmhouses.

The painters show deep theological insight when they place the great events of salvation in familiar landscapes close to home. People looking at the paintings will have the impression that these great mysteries are happening right in their own territory. When an artist paints an Annunciation scene, he makes sure to let us glimpse through an open window that this is happening right here in the town where he is painting. He wants us to recognize the familiar hills, the little bridge, and the city walls. When the shepherds come to visit the manger, the artist places the stable in his native Italy, in a spot just outside of Florence. Jesus, the painter is telling us, is born in our own midst. When Christ preaches his sermon on the Mount, he stands on a hill with the familiar bends of the Arno in the background, speaking to people who look like typical townsfolk of Tuscany.

These artists help us to do what Saint Benedict in his *Rule* asks his monks to do: "always be mindful of the presence of God." This mindfulness of God's constant, continuing presence in our lives is sometimes called the "fear of God." It doesn't mean cringing terror, but simply a clear awareness of this God who is present everywhere.

Dozens of chattering high schoolers pile onto the train, enlivening the dreary grown-up atmosphere with their rowdy laughing and loud kidding.

And then I realize something: the message of the great Italian masterpieces has gotten completely turned around. Ironically, for us citizens of the New World at least, the pictures do just the opposite of what their makers intended. They now encourage not the constant mindfulness of God's presence, but rather what Saint Benedict calls *oblivio*, forgetfulness.

These paintings assure us that God's great deeds were done in some place far, far away. Bethlehem, where God became flesh, is an unreal land of feather-shaped trees and castle-topped hills! The Christ child grew up in an idealized village in Tuscany—certainly nowhere around where I live. If the Way of the Cross winds through a quaint Italian town with a wall around it, then Jesus isn't likely to show up on my street in downtown Newark.

Some of us would prefer to forget that Jesus is present everywhere with his power and love, because that Jesus also has a way of making demands on us. We'd prefer God to be elsewhere, at some safe distance. If we keep Jesus slightly alien, we won't see him at our supper table or in our workplace. We won't have to hear his voice challenging us.

Across the aisle, a young mother holds her baby on her lap. At her feet is a diaper bag, and on the bench beside her is the baby's half-eaten cracker.

What would people think of a painting of Mary playing with Jesus not on an Italian hillside (which is somehow quite acceptable) but on the seat of a passenger train? Somehow it doesn't fit: Mary and Jesus don't have anything to do with the real mothers and real babies of today. God's love doesn't walk among us the way it did for Rafael and Michelangelo.

Benedict, who assumes that God is present everywhere, won't let the Lord be confined to churches, convents, and Vatican City—or even to some Renaissance landscape in Tuscany. He won't let God's great works be limited to "elsewhere." If we accept that Jesus healed lepers in Judea and in fifteenth-century Tuscany, we need to see him at work also in our own hospitals and sickrooms. If we can pray with great devotion in front of a painting of a Christ who is suffering and dying in the streets of some Italian village, Benedict wants us also to recognize him dying with heroin in his veins in the back alleys of our own cities. For Benedict it is decidedly not "somewhere else" that God works wonders.

Pontassieve. I shove myself and my suitcase down the aisle and squeeze through the knot of friendly teenagers smoking in the vestibule. They watch me climb awkwardly down the steep train steps. I land with a jolt on the platform in front of a handsome young man with long black hair who is waiting for the next train. I get a funny feeling as I look at him: hmm . . . where have I seen that face before?

Reflection

Where have you met Jesus in your life recently? In what kind of person is it easiest for you to recognize him? When is it hardest? Where are the places in which it is easiest for you to sense God's presence? Where is it most difficult? Ask the Lord to help you during Lent to cultivate a sense of the divine presence in that one person or place where it seems most difficult.

Sacred Scripture (Exod. 3:2–5, RSV)

And the angel of the LORD appeared to him in a flame of fire out of the midst of a bush; and he looked, and lo, the bush was burning, yet it was not consumed. And Moses said, "I will turn aside and see this great sight, why the bush is not burnt." When the LORD saw that he turned aside to see, God called to him out of the bush, "Moses, Moses!" And he said, "Here am I." Then he said, "Do not come near; put off your shoes from your feet, for the place on which you are standing is holy ground."

Rule of Benedict
(Chapter 19, "The Discipline of Psalmody," v. 1)

"We believe that the divine presence is everywhere and that in every place the eyes of the Lord are watching the good and the wicked."

Tuesday of the Fourth Week of Lent

Gödöllő, Hungary:
Welcoming the Guest

It's Christmas Eve, and for the first time in over thirty years, I'm not celebrating it in the monastery. Instead I'm holding the hand of Szófi, a bright, blonde five-year-old who is skipping and jumping on her way back from church after the traditional Christmas pageant. Her aunt, a friend of mine, is holding her other hand as we hurry through the cold Hungarian afternoon in Gödöllő, a small town twenty miles north of Budapest.

The parish church is actually the chapel of the famous Grassalkovich chateau, a great mansion that is being slowly restored after many years of abandonment and neglect. Built in 1744, the mansion was given in 1867 as a coronation present to the Emperor Franz Joseph I, who made it his family's summer residence. The baroque chapel of this "royal summer palace" was the setting for our afternoon's drama, with children playing all the roles. There was Mary, of course, and Joseph, the baby, and the shepherds. I think that Saint Francis of Assisi got involved, too, along with a couple of wicked robbers who, if I'm guessing correctly, were converted through the efforts of the saint.

The scheduling of the children's Christmas program for the afternoon of December 24 is carefully calculated. It's a convenient way to get the children out of the house so that "Baby Jesus and the angels" can come and put up the Christmas tree in the living room and set out the holiday presents. This year it is also a good way to arrange a few hours of quiet time for Szófi's mother who is due to give birth to her second child any time now.

On the walk home in the chilly, darkening afternoon we start to look into the windows of the austere Communist-era apartment buildings. Szófi spots the first Christmas tree, its colored electric lights sparkling gaily through the curtains of someone's second-floor apartment. She shouts excitedly and lets go of my hand to point at the window. I don't really need her aunt's translation: "She says that Jesus and the angels have visited that house over there." Soon we spot another lighted tree, and then another. "She says Baby Jesus has been all over Gödöllő this afternoon." And because of his visit these buildings seem brighter and happier places. Jumping with excitement, Szófi tries to get us to run. She can't wait to see her grandparents' apartment.

It's not too far now; she's pulling us along faster and faster. We keep spotting more Christmas trees through people's windows, more signs of Baby Jesus' presence.

At last we're in the hallway of the apartment building, and the delicious smells of Christmas cooking float down the stairs. When Grandpa opens the door for us, I don't understand his words, but I can guess from the tone of his voice and the shake of his head that Szófi's mom still hasn't had the baby. A question from Szófi draws a big smile from him. I recognize the Hungarian word "*Egen!*"—"Yes!" And the name "*Jesus.*" "Yes," he must be telling her, "Baby Jesus has been here and he's put the tree in the living room!" My five-year-old friend, bursting with curiosity, squirms impatiently as Grandpa finishes unbuttoning her coat. Finally free of his clutches, she scoots down the hall, leading Grandma, Grandpa, Aunt Babi, and me in an impromptu procession. I try to catch up to her before she turns the corner into the little living room—I want to watch the expression on her face when she sees that Baby Jesus has really come, just as he promised.

I catch up to her just in time to see her eyes fill with wonder. Jesus has actually come right into her grandparents' apartment this afternoon and made it a special, holy place! I start to hum to myself the words of an Advent carol:

Make your house fair as you are able,
Trim the hearth and set the table,
People look East, and sing to today,
Love, the guest, is on the way.

Szófi's delight makes me stop and ask myself what it would be like if we really took seriously the idea that Jesus was coming to our house as a guest. Would we have to scramble to make ourselves and our homes presentable? Would some favorite television programs have to be skipped to avoid embarrassing the Guest? Would there be more patience and fewer sarcastic remarks during family conversations?

Suddenly it dawns on me: "You know, she's right." When she peeks into the living room, Szófi sees the deeper truth that we grown-ups usually miss:

the Christmas tree and the presents so lovingly arranged by her grand-parents really *are* the handiwork of Jesus. This is no fairy tale, but a basic belief of our faith: love and selfless giving are not only signs, they are the actual presence of Christ in our midst. He is with us "wherever two or three are gathered" in his name. He is among us in the person of the poor, the oppressed, the child, the sick. He is present wherever there is self-giving love, kindness, or gentleness.

I need to learn from Szófi how to spot these presences everywhere and be cheered by them the way she is when she sees a Christmas tree glowing in someone's window.

Although this Christmas Eve isn't as solemn or silent as it would be in the monastery, it's teaching me to see the world once again the way little Szófi does. I glance at her grandparents and her aunt. They are still waiting in joyful hope for Marta to give birth. This Christmas, they can hardly wait to welcome God's grace and joy into their hearts and into their home—as a helpless newborn baby.

People look East, and sing to today,
Love, the guest, is on the way.

Reflection

Take a few moments to look at your life through the eyes of little Szófi, who sees the handiwork of Jesus all over the place. When has Jesus worked in your life through the loving actions of someone else? When have you done something that made Christ present for someone else?

A Lenten exercise: imagine that you want to prepare your heart to receive the risen Lord as a guest; think of three changes you might make in order to receive him more fittingly. What would you get rid of? What would you want to add or change?

Sacred Scripture (Luke 24:28–31, RSV)

So they drew near to the village to which they were going. He appeared to be going further, but they constrained him, saying, "Stay with us, for it is toward evening and the day is now far spent." So he went in to stay with them. When he was at table with them, he took the bread and blessed, and broke it, and gave it to them. And their eyes were opened and they recognized him.

Rule of Benedict
(Chapter 53, "The Reception of Guests," vv. 6–7)

"All humility should be shown in addressing a guest on arrival or departure. By a bow of the head or by a complete prostration of the body, Christ is to be adored because he is indeed welcomed in them."

Wednesday of the Fourth Week of Lent

Poitiers, France:
Encountering the Lord

To get to the city of Poitiers from the train station, I climb a long staircase that zigzags up the cliff behind which the town is presumably hiding. Out of breath at the top of the stairs, I find myself gaping up at the marvelous twelfth-century church of Saint Hilaire le Grand. It's named after Saint Hilary, bishop of Poitiers in the mid-300s, who wrote with deep insight about the mystery of the Holy Trinity and who successfully fended off the Arians by showing that Jesus was truly divine as well as truly human.

Florence 1450

A fifteen-minute walk through some thoroughly nondescript old streets brings me across town to a tiny but very venerable building that lies partially buried in the center of a busy traffic circle. This is the baptistery of Saint John, the oldest Christian structure in all of France, dating from about A.D. 290.

During my walk, I can't help thinking of a day in September of 1356 when the good citizens lined the tops of the town walls to watch the Battle of Poitiers. The vastly outnumbered English army crushed the French forces and headed for the coast, dragging with them as their prisoner the French king, Jean II, who was to fetch a hefty ransom.

I now find myself standing in the plaza in front of the city's jewel,

107

the church of Notre-Dame-la-Grande. Across its twelfth-century façade, fourteen carved saints stand solemnly in their niches, forever frozen in neat rows on either side of the central window. The paint that once enlivened the stone figures with bright colors has long since worn off, and the twelve apostles' features have weathered into a certain gray sameness that gives the whole group a pleasant unity.

Beneath this collection of saints, a strip of smaller carvings of bible stories stretches all the way across the façade. Toward its right-hand end I can make out scenes from the life of the Virgin Mary after whom the church is named. One of these catches my eye. What is she doing? Could it be? Yes! Here, in full view of staid, historic Poitiers, surrounded by the twelve apostles and two other saints, Mary of Nazareth is giving her baby a bath!

Saint Hilary, bishop of Poitiers, had doggedly defended the doctrine that Jesus was God, yet here the Divine Word stands hidden to his little waist in a big bathtub with his mother holding him up by the arms. Actually the image of God getting shampoo in his eyes doesn't shock me. After all, we Christians meditate daily on far worse things than that happening to Jesus. No, what unsettles me is the idea of Mary getting splashed.

I've visited many of the great museums of the Western world, and I've thumbed through books of Christian art for decades, so I think I know how this is supposed to work. Mary is to be found praying in her room, or kneeling in awed adoration beside the manger. She weeps in silent dignity at the foot of the cross or sits in marble coldness holding her dead son on her lap. She rides on the clouds of heaven or is crowned by Christ in glory. At her most undignified, she's sometimes caught riding a donkey. But I've never seen a picture of Mary getting the washcloth thrown in her face or grabbing for the bottle of baby oil just as the Christ child is about to toss it into the tub.

As I watch, Mary lets go of one of the divine wrists to push a few stray hairs back under her veil; the baby takes quick advantage to reach down with his fat little hand and slap at the water. His mother, naturally, gets splashed full in the face—a treatment familiar to millions of mothers before and since. With a look of startled surprise, she stares down at her soaked dress. Clucking her tongue in mild exasperation she tries to grab the slippery arm before more damage is done. I notice for the first time how much the squirming little boy looks like his mother, especially around the mouth and eyes. Her futile attempts to capture the offending arm quickly become a playful contest between mother and baby, and their laughter carries across the church plaza. Delighted with the new game, he slaps a fistful of bath water up at the dignified Saint Peter who is standing nearby holding two big keys. By this time all the saints in their colorful robes are looking down at the scene and laughing. Peter is roaring with delight as he dries off the keys to the kingdom.

Suddenly façade is gray, lifeless stone again. What have I just seen? It must have been some devilish delusion. Surely Mary, whom the litany calls "Tower of Ivory" and "Ark of the Covenant," Mary, the Queen of Heaven, never put on an apron, rolled back those flowing white sleeves, and gave her baby a bath!

This simple little scene in Poitiers is a powerful reminder of a basic Christian principle, and one central to Benedict's vision: the bath is sacred because God is present there. We should expect to bump into God in just such ordinary places. A God who can fit into a baby's bathtub can surely fit into a kitchen, a classroom, an office, or a shopping mall.

My train leaves in half an hour, and it's a long walk back to the station. Reluctantly I turn and head across the plaza. Just before rounding the corner I sneak a last quick glance over my shoulder. There are the apostles, standing stony and stiff again. There is the Blessed Mother in the lowest row, off to the right, still giving the Son of God his bath. But I swear her dress looks wet.

Reflection

Part of the conversion experience is an increased awareness of the divine presence all around us. Take a few minutes to sit quietly in your kitchen, your bedroom, or your work place. Do you feel the presence of God there? Don't try to force the experience, but just relax and ask the Lord to speak to you in that place.

Do you really believe that when you're bathing the baby or filling out your income tax forms you are answering your unique call to holiness? During this holy season ask the Lord to help you experience your state of life as your personal and unique path to holiness; ask for the grace to see Jesus as he walks with you on each step of the journey

Sacred Scripture (Matt. 13:54–57, RSV)

And coming to his own country [Jesus] taught them in their synagogue, so that they were astonished, and said, "Where did this man get this wisdom and these mighty works? Is not this the carpenter's son? Is not his mother called Mary? And are not his brothers James and Joseph and Simon and Judas? And are not all his sisters with us? Where then did this man get all this?" And they took offense at him.

Rule of Benedict
(Chapter 31, "Qualifications of the Monastery Cellerar," v. 10)

"[The cellerar] will regard all utensils and goods of the monastery as sacred vessels of the altar."

Thursday of the Fourth Week of Lent

Brussels, Belgium:
Noticing God

The Musée d'Art Ancien, the national art museum in Brussels, is filled, as I expected, with a spectacular collection of Flemish and Dutch paintings. I wander past masterpieces by Frans Hals, Rembrandt, and Van Dyck: portraits of well-fed merchants wearing wide lace collars and self-satisfied smiles. I gape at the weird prophetic fantasies of Hieronymus Bosch, whose strange goblin creatures ride on the backs of pterodactyls and toss bombs onto the bizarre blue landscape far below.

I'm here in search of my favorite painting, by Peter Bruegel the Elder. I come at last into a room full of paintings by the two Bruegels, father and son, and easily recognize the charming rural scenes and the brown, gray, and russet earth tones of the elder Bruegel. I pause in front of his "The Slaughter of the Holy Innocents."

Bruegel has set the biblical story in his own country and his own century: the occupying troops are not Roman legionnaires but Spanish soldiers. I watch in fascinated horror as men in silver breastplates and helmets raid a country village in Bruegel's native Flanders. Under the approving eye of their commander, they are stabbing little babies as terrified mothers scream in horror and try in vain to protect their children. The painter's own pain and sorrow give the scene more realism and emotional impact than any other depiction of this story I've ever seen.

Since this is in fact the companion piece to my favorite painting, I scan the other walls expectantly. Soon I begin to worry that the picture I've come to see may be out on loan or temporarily removed for restoration. With fingers crossed I move on into the next room, where, according to the sign, there are more Bruegels. Turning to my left, I break into a relieved smile as I recognize my old familiar friend: "The Numbering at Bethlehem."

The canvas, about six feet long and three-and-a-half feet high, depicts a snowy winter scene in a busy little sixteenth-century Flemish village. The painting is buzzing with the activities of daily life: chickens are scratching the snow for food, children are playing on the ice and throwing snowballs, a butcher is slaughtering a pig in front of his shop, men are warming themselves around an outdoor fire, and a young man is courting a maid as they skate on the river. Off to the left, people cluster patiently in the cold as an official at an open window writes their names in a fat book.

This is the painter's interpretation of the scene in Bethlehem as Jews "from the House of David" came to register for the census decreed by Caesar Augustus. Bruegel and his countrymen in sixteenth-century Brabant could identify with the Jews of Jesus' time. The Netherlands was suffering under the oppressive rule of the king of Spain in the same way that Judea had once shivered in the ominous shadow of the Emperor of Rome who had ordered the census.

Searching carefully among the tiny, busy figures near the center of the picture, I pick out a brown-robed man. The large saw he is carrying over his shoulder shows that he is a carpenter. He's leading a little gray donkey on which is seated a young woman bundled in a blue blanket. I can feel the sharp cold on my cheeks and hear the delighted shrieks of the children and the squeal of the unfortunate pig. The smell of wood smoke sours the air. As the couple and their donkey trudge wearily past me in the snow, I notice that the young woman, who is obviously pregnant, looks drawn and tired. No one in the village is paying the least attention to them. The children are absorbed in their play, the butchers and the merchants are going about their business, and the grim-faced officials are taking their census. The carpenter turns the donkey toward the crowded inn. A sad sun hangs like a frozen orange in the black skeleton of a tree.

Two other visitors to the museum pause beside me for a moment to glance casually at the painting. I ask myself, "Do they see Joseph and Mary? What if they don't know enough to look for the man with the saw and the girl on the donkey?" I'm bursting to poke one of them and whisper, "Psst! Do you see them? They're right there, in the middle, next to the man at the big wine barrel!" But I hold myself back, and in a few seconds the visitors move on.

Peter Bruegel's painting reminds us that Christmas is a very subtle feast—a celebration of God's bashful, self-giving love and infinite humility. The dull, understated colors in the painting convey this subtlety so perfectly that tourists in the museum look right at the picture without seeing what it is really about. It is, of course, about love, Love that became a human being and dwelt among us. But love comes quietly, even mysteriously sometimes. The scene of the poor Flemish village occupied by foreign troops reminds us that God, like love itself, is somehow linked with the mystery of human suffering and the shadowy side of life. We can almost hear the oppressed villagers in the painting complaining, at the very moment that the couple with the donkey walks past them, "Where is God? Why is God so far away and unconcerned about our lives?"

This is why the holiday season always brings that awful letdown, that almost inevitable sense of disappointment. It is not simply because reality can never live up to our idealized childhood memories or the romanticized scenes of Christmas we see on television. A more fundamental reason lies in the mystery of Christmas itself: after all of the "hype" from the Old Testament prophets about the future Prince of Peace, after all of the Advent preparation for the coming of the "Desire of Nations," Salvation finally arrives and what do we see? Just a tired couple with a baby. God has come to save us, sure, but as nothing more than an infant, a bundle of possibility, powerless and mute, vulnerable and unrecognizable. This is the built-in disappointment of Christmas. But this is also its greatness.

It is only in coming as a baby that God can assure the powerless that salvation doesn't lie in might and mastery. It is only by being born in a stable that God can persuade the poor that salvation doesn't lie in wealth and economic security. It is only by being born unnoticed in the obscurity of a small town that the King of Kings can convince the unloved that our salvation doesn't lie in fame or popularity. Emmanuel, God-with-us, comes as Mystery to be seen only with the eyes of faith. God comes as a surprise, in a shocking reversal of this world's wisdom.

Emmanuel enters the cold, busy villages of our lives all the time, often unfelt and unrecognized, the way the carpenter and his wife slip into this Flemish hamlet in the snow. In fact, it is one of Benedict's great spiritual principles that Christ is present in everyone around us. When I walk into a hospital room to offer a cheering word to a depressed patient, Emmanuel is using my voice to come as the healer of the sick. When a busy parent takes the time to sit down and go over a third-grader's homework with her, this is Christ, Wisdom from on high, coming to earth. When someone refuses to join in an office joke that degrades women or some racial minority, the Sun of Justice is dawning a little more in our world.

A man in a dark blue suit walks into the center of the room and announces in a commanding voice that the museum is closing in a few minutes and everyone has to leave. I take one final look at my favorite painting: a gray afternoon in a rundown village. Just for practice I search the busy scene one more time, looking for the young couple and their donkey.

Reflection

The discipline of Lent sharpens your ability to notice when God shows up. It also makes you more willing and able to let Jesus use your hands and your voice so that he can become present to people in the world. Think of someone in particular for whom you could be the presence of Christ through your kindness or your help.

Sacred Scripture (Gal. 2:20, RSV)

"It is no longer I who live, but Christ who lives in me."

Rule of Benedict
(Chapter 53, "The Reception of Guests," v. 1)

"All guests who present themselves are to be welcomed as Christ, for he himself will say: I was a stranger and you welcomed me.'"

Friday of the
Fourth Week of Lent

Saint Malo, France:
Giving Thanks

Père Michel, the local parish priest, is giving me an evening tour of the narrow streets of his native Saint Malo. This small port town is a peninsula wrapped in 1,900 meters of stone ramparts and fifteen centuries of sea lore. Her sturdy houses of tan granite, with their steeply pitched slate roofs and dormer windows, tower above the tops of the battlements as if watching the fishing boats in the bay. Due west, over the horizon, is Great Britain.

Saint Malo is a seafarers' city whose intrepid explorers and merchants sailed their three-masted Cap-horniers to every part of the globe. They brought back goods and tall tales from Africa and Antarctica, New Orleans and New Zealand, China, and Argentina. This is the home port of Jacques Cartier, who set off from here on his first voyage of exploration to Canada in 1534.

Inside the town walls this evening, the smell of the sea and the romance of the sailing days still reach into every corner. My priest-guide, who is practicing his English on me, keeps up an interesting monologue about the history of his town. In the late 1600s, he tells me, corsairs from Saint Malo put to sea in their light, swift ships to wreak havoc on English shipping in the name of the king of France. In their heyday, they once captured 3,800 commercial vessels in the space of ten years. It's no wonder the English called Saint Malo a "hornet's nest."

We're now strolling through a corner of the town where the buildings date back to those days. You can still see five-story houses of wood and stone, with bizarre angles at their corners. Crooked chimneys, topped with quaint red chimney pots, sprout up randomly in a rolling sea of slate roofs. Up and down the eight-foot-wide streets, the old houses lean into one another in charming disorder, as if jostling and kidding together.

Space was already at a premium even back when these houses were built, so they were made high and narrow, with stingy spiral staircases inside and narrow air shafts for ventilation and sunlight. Residents of these wooden buildings slept with their fingers crossed, knowing that the shops and warehouses next door on either side were bulging with tallow, tar, and gunpowder for the tall ships.

I'm now under the spell of Père Michel's stories. My fellow tourists start to look like rough sailors, leathery old sea captains, and swaggering corsairs. They're shouting to one another about the latest exploits of Duguay-Trouin, the first great corsair captain, who has just captured a dozen more English ships this week. I smell pots of molten tar and the smoke from wood chip fires used to treat the bottoms of the ships. Busy merchant establishments, ship chandlers, and taverns are all crowded together along stinking, muddy streets.

The priest stops at a small wooden door, takes out a key, and lets us through. We begin to wind our way along dark, silent hallways and upward through a warren of little rooms in the Catholic high school where he teaches and lives. He shows me some arches and stone walls dating back over 800 years. These, he explains, once belonged to a Benedictine monastery. I feel at home now.

As we climb a fourth flight of dark, squeaky stairs, he tells me, "Actually, we're climbing up here just to watch the sun set. Saint Malo is famous for her sunsets, you know!" He leads me to a small closed window high above the western ramparts.

In the foreground beneath us the battlements, towers, and turrets loom in the lengthening shadows.

This would have been the hour when lanterns were hoisted high by ropes on pulleys to light the narrow streets. In medieval days the curfew bell, *la noguette*, was rung at 10:00 p.m., and the town gates were shut tight. From the late sixteenth century through the eighteenth, the streets were patrolled after dark by a unique police force: about fifty vicious mastiffs. These huge dogs that had been starved during the day were let out to roam the city streets after curfew and were recalled in early morning by the sound of a copper trumpet. In 1770, a poor sailor was coming home late and was caught by these canine "police." The grisly evidence was found scattered around the town next morning. Many an unlucky thief must have met swift justice this way over the centuries.

I'm pulled back into the present by the squawking of seagulls that wheel in graceful circles just outside our window. Beyond the dark ramparts, I can make out a ribbon of deserted sand and the gray line of gentle soundless surf. Near the shore three rocky islets lurk in the shallow waves like beached sea monsters. Farther out in the bay, fiery flickers of setting sun dance on the silken wrinkles of the gulf of Saint Malo. We watch in silence as the orange sun slips reverently below the horizon. Neither of us is willing to break the spell cast by the breathtaking beauty of this everyday event. I mutter a quiet, heartfelt prayer of thanks for the splendor of the spectacle I'm watching.

In the monastery we cultivate a sense of awareness of God by starting and ending everything with a prayer: community meetings, for example, and table reading, and the lessons at the Liturgy of the Hours in church.

The custom of praying grace before and after meals gets you in the habit of being thankful to God not just for food but for everything you have. You can thank God for a cool evening breeze, the rough texture of a sweater, the sparkle in a baby's eyes, or the bright face of a sophomore in the second row.

Why not say grace before receiving these other gifts from God? Grace before listening to Mozart? Grace before jumping into the pool on a hot day? Grace before opening the door to my cousin and her little children who've come to visit? Grace at my desk before starting my daily job (thankful, perhaps, that I have a job to do)?

If I thank God after a meal because I recognize it as a gift, then why not a sincere grace after seeing the face of a particularly pretty girl? Or grace after a difficult but fruitful meeting? Grace after helping a slow student master a tricky French verb?

If everything is a grace and a gift, then why not say grace even on unpleasant occasions, in times of suffering, knowing that hidden inside of the pain is a mysterious gift from a loving God? Grace during an illness? Grace after a disagreement?

It's dark now, and Père Michel and I are still standing at our window. The last few gulls have gone home for the night. The sea is a rippling veil of black satin. The Bidouane tower broods over the ghostly ramparts below. Its pointed slate roof starts to tingle with the first flecks of silver as the moon comes up behind us. A silent prayer forms in my heart: grace before moonrise. . . .

Reflection

Many people used to make pilgrimages as a way of showing gratitude to God for some favor received. Make a list of things and people you are thankful for. Try to think of a few for which you have never explicitly thanked God before. As you go down your list, try to think of an appropriate way to show your gratitude to the Lord for each gift.

Sacred Scripture (1 Thess. 5:16–18)

"Rejoice always, pray without ceasing, give thanks in all circumstances."

Rule of Benedict
(Chapter 57, "The Artisans of the Monastery," v. 9)

". . . so that in all things God may be glorified."

Saturday of the
Fourth Week of Lent

Assisi, Italy:
Speaking of God

A mile and a half of wet, black road stretches in front of me like a shiny sword pointing to the medieval hilltop town ahead. Menacing gray clouds swirl low over the flat farmland beneath Assisi. The thirty-minute walk takes me alongside furrowed fields that sleep in the chilly drizzle and dream of sunshine and clear summer skies.

assisi

In 1203 Francesco Bernardone, the son of a cloth merchant, known for his high-spirited and worldly ways, suddenly renounced all of his possessions and his former life in order to take the gospel literally. Although he had no intention at all of founding a religious order, Francis soon attracted likeminded men to his new way of living the gospel. The rest of his short life (he died at fourty-four) was a marvelous mixture of joyful poverty, prayer, preaching, and suffering both physical and spiritual. An extraordinary young noblewoman of Assisi, Clare, was inspired by his vision and became his follower and friend, ultimately founding an order of women based on Francis's principles.

The town on the high hillside keeps getting closer. At its very top, the old fort sits like a retired soldier—sodden, sad, and obsolete. Halfway down, medieval town walls slice across the face of the hill. Within five minutes I'm through the fortified town gate and walking around inside old Assisi. The guidebook makes a fuss over the great basilicas built to honor Saint Francis and his spiritual sister, Saint Clare. These churches are lovely, of course, but what really captivates me is the old town itself, which dates from the time of the two saints.

I wander through the maze of narrow streets connected by steep stairways. Cobblestone alleys wind between shuttered stone houses, beside terraces and beneath retaining walls. The medieval roadways, glowing silver in the drizzle, are barely wide enough for the little European cars that scuttle up and down the hill. I find myself standing in front of a building whose ground floor is now a small oratory. This, a sign tells me, is the site of the cloth-merchant establishment run by Francis's father. The living quarters upstairs are where the future saint was born and raised.

It takes very little imagination to picture the youthful Francesco and his friends strolling along these same steep streets singing and carousing and keeping an eye out for the young ladies. I can hear the jangle of swords and armor, and the clatter of horses' hooves as a band of warriors thunders out of the town gate to join in the almost constant warfare against one neighboring city or another.

Under my dripping umbrella, I weave my way across the face of the hillside through streets and alleys and up flights of slippery stone steps, meeting only an occasional hardy pedestrian. February isn't a bad time to see Assisi, I think to myself, if you like to be alone.

I stop for a few moments at the edge of a terrace that overlooks the valley. Far below, in the misty gray distance, lies the tiny train station and, farther still, the overly solemn silhouette of Santa Maria dei Angeli, which houses Francis's little Portiuncula chapel. In the foreground, just beneath me at the foot of a sloped retaining wall, lies a soggy little terrace garden asleep in the winter rain. Near its outer edge is a small tree about ten feet tall. It doesn't seem to be a fruit tree as far as I can see. Maybe a nut tree?

Ah! Maybe it's the almond tree! I smile as I remember the story from the *Fioretti*, a collection of edifying legends about the deeds of the wonder-worker Francis. On a cold winter's day not unlike this one, the tale goes, Francis stopped in front of a bare almond tree and said, "Sister almond tree, speak to me of God!" And with that, the almond tree burst into a mass of lovely blossoms.

Francis was already in the habit of letting the creatures of nature or the events of daily life speak to him about God. This was his way of praying constantly, of staying in touch with God in every waking moment. So when the saint saw a bleak bare tree shivering in the drizzle, he just naturally asked it to say something to him about God. And in response, the Lord let the tree speak eloquently to Francis about the Lord's fruitful, joyous, and overflowing love for the world.

The practice of *lectio divina* teaches you to say, "Speak to me of God." As you read the sacred text, you keep asking yourself, "What does this word, phrase, or story say to my life here and now? What is God trying to say to me through this word?" As you get in the habit of asking that question about Scripture passages, you start asking it about events in your life: what is this particular experience saying to me? What is God telling me through this particular emotion?

It's not easy to look at a bleak situation or a deep disappointment the way Francis would have, or to invite a piece of bad news to "speak to me of God." When my carefully laid plans go awry, I don't always remember right away to ask the calamity to speak a word to me about God's care and concern.

The winter rain is thumping on my umbrella and cascading down the streets. Cool water is now seeping into my shoes.

"Speak to me of God!" Isn't it the job of every Christian to do that for others? For better or for worse, we tell one another about God all the time without even realizing it. We speak about God without opening our mouths, by a compassionate smile, a conscientiously prepared class, or a thoughtful gesture to a stranger in a crowded supermarket aisle. What are the chances that by watching me a person can learn that God is love? Do my actions with my fellow workers speak to them of a God who is infinitely patient and slow to anger? Has a student in trouble ever walked out of my office after a talk with me saying to himself, "How beautiful God must be!"

My fingers are cold and numb from holding the umbrella. I shiver as I think what a bad impression of God some folks have gotten because of my indifference or impatience. On the other hand I console myself with a lesson that I have learned over the years from countless brothers and sisters, friends and family members. Their acts of patience and forgiveness have spoken to me of God and said, "Even if you're not always what you could be, God is always compassionate and kind, slow to anger and rich in mercy!"

My feet are now soaking. Time to get indoors and dry out for a while. As I take a last look at the stark, black branches scratching against the gray sky I promise myself to return one day under a warm summer sun—to see if that little tree has almonds.

Reflection

Lent invites us to spend extra time in quiet prayer and meditating on Scripture. Choose a passage from the Bible, perhaps one assigned by the Church for this day, and as you slowly read it, ask the Lord to let a word or a phrase speak to your heart.

Think of a recent event in your life and ask it to speak to you of God. See what it might teach you about the Lord's love for you, or about your relationship with God.

Sacred Scripture (Hosea 14:5–6)

"He shall blossom like the lily. . . . His beauty shall be like the olive tree, and his fragrance like that of Lebanon."

Wisdom of the Desert

"A certain philosopher asked Saint Antony: Father, how can you be so happy when you are deprived of the consolation of books? Antony replied: 'My book, O philosopher, is the nature of created things, and any time I want to read the words of God, the book is before me.'"[4]

---

4. Thomas Merton, trans., *The Wisdom of the Desert: Sayings from the Desert Fathers of the Fourth Century* (New York: New Direction Books, 1970), 67–68.

THE FIFTH WEEK
OF LENT

Hoping in the Lord

In the desert Israel had to depend on God for everything: military protection, food, water, and guidance through the trackless waste. On our own life's journey we have to learn to rely on God rather than on substitutes. Toward the end of Lent, the Church's lectionary readings show us the sinister forces gathering against Jesus, and his growing awareness of his impending death. At the same time they show him relying more and more on his Father. In the end, on Calvary, he will let go of everything until he has absolutely nothing left. Nothing but his trust in God.

The chapters for this week, then, dwell on our response to Jesus' example of confident dependence on God alone. "Lérins" assures us that God's love keeps sustaining us at every moment of our lives. "Loch Ness" celebrates the experience of hoping in the midst of adversity. "Ligugé" reminds us that it is especially in times of trouble that, like Jesus, we can to turn to God in prayer. "Chambord" meditates on the gift of perspective, which allows us to see God's plan at work in our lives. "Amsterdam" insists on the need to confidently face and accept the mystery of suffering, just as Jesus did. Finally, "Saint Gervais" offers the example of one courageous woman's unshakeable trust in divine providence.

Monday of the Fifth Week of Lent

Lérins, France:
Drinking from the River

The monks' white-and-blue boat is a sturdy little converted fishing craft. Perched on a hard bench inside its bare cabin, I watch through square, spray-spattered windows as the city of Cannes rolls and pitches, fading into the morning mist.

The choppy sea tosses our boat in three directions at once. I quickly learn from my two fellow passengers how to prop my feet and elbows to keep from being suddenly launched through a window and into the whitecaps. Now that I'm properly braced I can take my mind off of simple survival and think about where I'm heading. The monastery of Lérins on the island of Saint Honorat is a very special place for me as a monk.

Except for a brief period after the French Revolution, Saint Honorat has been a monks' island for almost 1,600 years. About the year A.D. 400, a certain Honoratus arrived with a few companions in search of a secluded place in which to practice a new, experimental form of Christian life called monasticism. They settled on the snake-infested wilderness islet called Lerina and turned it into one of the great centers of monastic life in Europe. The successors of Honoratus renamed the island in his name, and tended it lovingly into a garden spot. Here they wrote some of the early monastic "Rules" in the West (Saint Benedict wouldn't be born for another eighty years) and trained missionaries for England and Ireland (including Saint Benedict Biscop and perhaps even Saint Patrick). Their community provided many holy bishops for the cities of Gaul—most notably Honoratus himself and a special favorite of mine, Saint Caesarius of Arles.

Careful to hold on to the wooden bench with both hands, I twist around to look out the front window. There it is, straight ahead, a tiny, tree-covered island lying low against the pink and tan clouds of the Mediterranean sunrise.

About the year 490, Caesarius, by now Bishop of Arles, wrote in a sermon to his brethren back on the island:

> O happy isle of Lerina, which, while seeming small and flat to the eye, has nevertheless lifted countless mountain peaks toward the sky. It is she who forms eminent monks and provides such remarkable bishops to all the provinces.

I'm very conscious of this sense of tradition as I step off the boat in the quiet cove and begin a half-mile walk to the monastery of Lérins. The dirt road takes me past a stone hermit chapel, between hushed fields where scrubby lavender bushes rest in neat rows, then past quiet work-shops and outbuildings. I remember that it was the monks of Lérins who developed a concept new to Western monastic thinking—the importance of manual labor. Earlier monastic founders in Europe such as Martin of Tours would not allow their monks to work at all so that they could be free to pray constantly. But on Lérins the monks believed in the ideal of a balance between work and prayer. As I walk past the island's well-tended gardens, fields, and vineyards, it's clear that the tradition is still flourish-ing today. I finally reach the monastery buildings. The whole island radi-ates peace and welcome, but this is especially true of the Cistercian monks themselves, who greet me warmly and make me feel at home right away.

Saint Honorat Island is only about 800 yards long and 500 yards wide, and it takes less than forty-five minutes to follow its shoreline in a com-plete circle. During one such walk the next afternoon, I notice its larger sister-island, Saint Catherine, across a narrow channel, and remember why the early monks had chosen the present island instead of the larger one. I heard the explanation just that morning.

The story begins back on the mainland, far up in the hills behind Cannes, where a little river starts on its way to the sea. But after some miles, it suddenly disappears underground, flowing under the mountains, beneath the shoreline, and below the seabed itself. It crosses under the Bay of Cannes, bypassing Saint Catherine but flowing beneath Saint Honorat before emptying its fresh water somewhere farther out in the Mediterranean. What had made the monks choose the little island over its larger partner, then, was its supply of fresh water. The underground river provided "sweet water flowing amid the bitterness of the sea." It was this that had allowed the monks to turn their rocky islet into a fruitful garden.

The next morning I stand outside the monastery, watching the sun rise over the pink spray of the waves that splash on the rocks. We've been up for a couple of hours. The gentle daily routine begins at 3:30 a.m. with Vigils and continues through periods of quiet and community prayer, reading, meals, and work in the vineyard, the library, the kitchen, or one of the workshops. But Saint Honorat has not always been this peaceful.

It seems that over the centuries there were constant raids, whether from pirates, Saracens, the Spanish, or the Genoese. Near one of the ancient hermit chapels researchers recently discovered a *martyrium*, the burial place of several monks killed during one of the frequent raids in the early days. And out on a rocky point nearby, past the *martyrium* and the seaside chapel, a strange granite box of a building stares outward across the waves. This was a unique response to the problem of security: a windowless stone cube that served as a four-story fortified monastery. Although the monastery-fort was abandoned quite a while ago, the bad times continued. In more recent years, the island monks have had to put up with cannons being placed on top of their hermit chapels and having troops billeted on their sacred soil.

Throughout all of these trials, however, the underground river kept flowing. When the gardens ran red with the blood of brothers slain by marauders, the river still ran clean. When the abbot had to travel to Spain to ransom two of his novices from the Saracens, the river still flowed fresh. When the ancient stone walls of a sacred hermit chapel collapsed under the weight of a clumsy cannon squatting on its roof, the hidden river kept running cool, year after year.

The life of every baptized Christian is like this islet. Each of us has a spiritual stream of grace, a river of God's love flowing beneath our everyday existence, constantly giving us life and making us fruitful and beautiful.

It flows below the busy surface of our daily routine and deep beneath our pains and pleasures, hopes and struggles, making all of these bear fruit.

In that same sermon, Saint Caesarius, perhaps remembering the cool water of the underground river, writes to the monks of his beloved Lerina:

> See, I am preparing the reservoir of my heart to receive the divine waters which flow through you. For I really know you well, and it is about you that we read this word of the Savior, "He who believes in me, rivers of living water will flow from his breast." . . . We joyfully believe that living waters flow from you like spiritual fountains.

This is one of those typical thought-provoking images that fill Caesarius's writings: we need to stay in touch with that faithful stream, to keep drinking from that well of eternal life, not just for ourselves, but so that we can in turn become sources of life for those around us.

The bell for Lauds is wafting across the island, borne on the crisp January sea wind. As I hurry to prayers, I pass an empty garden patch and notice how bare the soil looks. I'm comforted, though, by the thought that at this very moment, deep beneath the barren fields, life is still flowing in the hidden, changeless river.

Reflection

Water is a very ancient Lenten symbol, referring to the water God gave the Israelites in the desert, and especially to the waters of Baptism that the catechumens will receive at the Easter Vigil. Jesus once said "If any one thirst, let him come to me and drink. He who believes in me, as the Scripture has said, 'Out of his heart shall flow rivers of living water.'" (John 7:37–38) Are there times when you feel cut off from Christ, who is the water of life?

In what ways do you experience God's river of grace constantly flowing beneath your life? What might you do to let that stream flow more easily? How might you be a fountain of life-giving water for someone around you today?

Sacred Scripture (John 4:7–10, RSV)

There came a woman of Samaria to draw water. Jesus said to her, "Give me a drink." For his disciples had gone away into the city to buy food. The Samaritan woman said to him, "How is it that you, a Jew, ask a drink of me, a woman of Samaria?" For Jews have no dealings with Samaritans. Jesus answered her, "If you knew the gift of God, and who it is that is saying to you, 'Give me a drink,' you would have asked him, and he would have given you living water."

Rule of Benedict (Prologue, v. 49)

"As we progress in this way of life and in faith, we shall run on the path of God's commandments, our hearts overflowing with the inexpressible delight of love."

Tuesday of the
Fifth Week of Lent

Loch Ness, Scotland:
Finding Hope

This morning, a cold rain crackled for hours against the dark window-pane of the guest room in the monastery of Fort Augustus. This after-noon, then, I'm glad for the invitation to climb the stairs of the abbey's bell tower with a brother who has to change the measurement card in the sunlight recorder. (The Royal Weather Service once reported that this village has fewer hours of sunshine per year than any town in the United Kingdom.) We're on the narrow stone steps that wind steeply upward inside the square tower. I clutch the hem of my black Benedictine habit in one hand to keep from tripping on it, and I start remembering what I've read about the geology of these Scottish Highlands.

Between three and four hundred million years ago, in a succession of tremors, Scotland cracked open along a diagonal fault running across the whole island from northeast to southwest. The northern part slowly slid southwest some sixty-five miles. Then, more recently (somewhere between ten and twenty-five thousand years ago), glaciers four thousand feet thick scoured the open wound and shaped it into what is called on the map "The Great Glen." Today the Glen includes a lake twenty-two miles long, a mile-and-a-half wide at its widest, and 700 feet deep for most of its length. Tree-clad mountains rise 2,000 feet on either side of this, the largest freshwater lake in Great Britain and the third deepest in Europe. This is Loch Ness.

At the southwestern end of the Loch, where the River Oich empties in, lies the hamlet of Fort Augustus. In the 1700s, the English king put a fort here to control the clans and subdue the proud Highlanders. On the site today stands the Benedictine monastery of Fort Augustus Abbey where I'm staying for the week. It's this monastery's tower that I'm climb-ing right now.

We're at the top of the stairs already. While the brother sets about replacing the little cardboard disc in the sunlight recorder inside the tower, I step through a low doorway and out onto the walkway that circles the tower high above Loch Ness. I rest my elbows on the rough stone parapet and take in the scene below.

The rain has stopped, except for an occasional stray drop that glints in the fickle sunlight. Gray, frayed clouds and a few tattered rags of blue sky hang over the brooding black of the loch. Steep mountainsides of gold, brown, green, and burgundy stretch quietly along both sides of the narrow lake to disappear in the dim distance. Straight ahead, in the center of the scene, arching up out of the dark waters of Loch Ness in a gorgeous shimmering curve of colors, glows a shiny new rainbow. Like most really bright rainbows, this one almost seems to be giving off a quiet hum.

Everything is hushed except for the whisper of the rainbow and the whistle of the winter wind flapping my cassock around my knees. I'm struck by the unlikely contrast: the murky, mist-shrouded ink of Loch Ness and the sparkling colors of the rainbow.

The loch is famous for only one thing nowadays, of course—the notorious monster that shows itself every now and then, just often enough to keep scientists, writers, and tourists busy speculating. After breakfast this morning, old Father Gregory told me that he and a friend saw "Nessie" from the monastery's dock in 1971. The dark waters of Loch Ness have become a symbol of unsolved mystery: somewhere in their depths lurks a creature left over from the first days of creation when God made the sea monsters.

The story of the rainbow, like that of the creation of the sea monsters, goes back to the Book of Genesis. God has finished the work of creating the world, bringing order out of the primordial chaos, and sees that it is good. Then, not long afterward, the forces of disorder reenter the picture. There are signs that the order of creation is breaking down: the disobedience of Adam and Eve in eating of the forbidden fruit; the murder of Abel by his own brother, Cain; and the arrogant raising of the Tower of Babel toward heaven. Then, with the coming of the great flood, the world is finally plunged back again into complete chaos. When the waters have receded, Noah steps out of the ark, and God speaks to him, promising that never again will the dark powers of evil be allowed to overwhelm the earth. As the sign and guarantee of the divine promise the Lord fashions something brand new, a sort of supplement to the work of creation: the rainbow. This, the only thing God is said to have created outside the first six days, the Lord now places like a "bow in the clouds." To this day, the rainbow is the sign of God's vow to always control the forces of darkness, disorder, and chaos that keep trying to destroy our world.

You have to be in the right place at the right time to see a rainbow. First, you have to be in or near a rainstorm, under dark clouds. Second, you can't be facing the sun, enjoying its warmth on your face, but must have your back to it. It's a perfect sign of hope, a gift for people who are overshadowed by rain clouds in their lives, who are experiencing storms of discouragement, despair, or depression. It only appears to people who, for whatever reason, aren't looking toward the light. Perhaps they don't know which direction to look, or maybe they're angry and have turned their back on God. But it is then that they are candidates for a rainbow.

This winter rainbow leaps out of Loch Ness the way hope springs up in the midst of a painful mystery. The joyful bundle of light curves up from the murky Loch like new confidence suddenly bursting out of the depths of an unfathomable problem. The sunlight bounces off the rain-drops the way God's love sometimes shines through our tears to make a beautiful bow in the clouds, God's "I promise" holding good in the face of our personal chaos. The rainbow always appears sooner or later. Sometimes it seems late in coming, sometimes it's very faint, sometimes only a piece of it can be seen. You can get pretty skillful at finding rain-bows in clouds—but only if you're convinced from the start that the rain-bow is there somewhere.

"Well, Father, the sunshine recorder is reset. Oh, I say! You're looking a bit cold! Ready to come back inside?" It's my meteorologist guide popping his head out of the door. "Yes, thanks," I answer, stealing a last glance at the rainbow before I follow him inside.

Reflection

Are you someone who is "convinced from the start that the rainbow is there somewhere?" Prayer and *lectio* can help us to be more sensitive to the Lord's rainbows on our journey. Can you name a few signs of hope that God has offered you during difficult times (perhaps through giving you a faithful friend, a safe place, or a certain happy event)?

Sacred Scripture (Gen. 9:11–15, RSV)

[God said to Noah and to his sons] "I establish my covenant with you, that never again shall all flesh be cut off by the waters of a flood, and never again shall there be a flood to destroy the earth." And God said, "This is the sign of the covenant which I make between me and you and every living creature that is with you, for all future generations: I set my bow in the clouds, and it shall be a sign of the covenant between me and the earth. When I bring clouds over the earth and the bow is seen in the clouds, I will remember my covenant which is between me and you and every living creature of all flesh; and the waters shall never again become a flood to destroy all flesh."

Rule of Benedict
(Chapter 8, "The Procedure for Receiving Brothers," vv. 7–8)

"The concern must be whether the novice truly seeks God and whether he shows eagerness for the work of God, for obedience, and for trials. The novice should be clearly told all the hardships and difficulties that will lead him to God."

Wednesday of the Fifth Week of Lent

Ligugé, France: Passing through Fire

I'm speeding across the fertile farmland of France's Poitou region on the train from Paris to Bordeaux. We're about five minutes south of Poitiers when I look out the window to my left. The narrow, tree-lined canal that lies lazily alongside the tracks was built by the Romans when this was the province of Gallia. I look out the other side of the train just in time to glimpse a collection of stone buildings huddling around a church tower. This is the Benedictine Abbey of Ligugé, said to be the oldest monastery in the Western Christian world. Its story takes me on a trip back in time. . . .

Kirtgher Alsace

About the year A.D. 361, a strange young man in his late twenties took up residence in the ruins of an ancient Gallo-Roman villa on the site of the present monastery. He was born in Pannonia (present-day Hungary) but was raised in Italy. At the age of fifteen, he had been forced by law to follow in the footsteps of his father, who was an officer in the Roman army. Three years later, he was baptized a Christian and soon became a disciple of Hilary, the saintly bishop of nearby Poitiers.

Well-known for his holiness of life even before his baptism, over time the young man would become more and more famous for the countless miraculous cures he performed. As so often happens to holy men in the fourth century, he would eventually be drafted by the people to become bishop of their town.

As Bishop of Tours, he became an energetic foe of the pagan cults that still flourished in the Roman Empire at the time. His fame as a miracle worker spread across Gaul, and by the time of his death he was already being honored as "Saint Martin of Tours." Many paintings and statues recall the famous story of his cutting his soldier's cloak down the middle in order to give half of it to a beggar. The next night, the story goes, Jesus appeared to Martin clothed in the cloak he'd given to the poor man.

In the earliest biography of Saint Martin, Sulpicius Severus gives a long and impressive list of the monk-bishop's wonderful deeds to prove that Martin was a perfect saint whom God protected from all harm. After the *Life of St. Martin* was published, however, Sulpicius felt he had to write a letter to a certain Eusebius to defend Martin from slander: there was a story going around alleging that the supposedly invulnerable Martin had once been burned in a fire. Here is the story that Sulpicius retells.

Martin is making the rounds of the parishes in his diocese and decides to sleep in a little room attached to the church he is visiting. He is uncomfortable with the luxury of the straw mattress that has been made up for him and so pushes the straw aside and sleeps on the wooden floor. During the night, a defective stove used for heating the room sets fire to the straw and Martin is awakened around midnight by a cloud of thick, choking smoke. He gropes his way quickly to the door and begins pulling frantically on the bolt to unlock it. The bolt won't budge! Within a few moments, flames fill the room and engulf the bishop, singeing the hem of his robe. Weak with fear, he struggles again with the stubborn bolt. Still no luck! I'll let Sulpicius finish the story in his own flowery style:

> At length recovering his habitual conviction that safety lay not in flight but in the Lord, and seizing the shield of faith and prayer, committing himself entirely to the Lord, he lay down in the midst of the flames. Then indeed, the fire having been removed by divine intervention, he continued to pray amid a circle of flames that did him no harm.

By Martin's own admission, he had taken longer than he should have to turn to the power of prayer. He'd been startled out of a sound sleep to find himself in terrible danger. The saint later spoke of this incident as a snare that the devil had laid for him, a snare that, for a moment, had worked.

Sulpicius is truly indignant when people imply that this scene shows some imperfection in Martin. "This event which is ascribed to the infirmity of Martin," he argues, "is, in reality, full of dignity and glory, since indeed, being tried by a most dangerous calamity, he came forth a conqueror."

The story certainly does end in dignity and glory, but maybe Christians would be better served by meditating on what the good bishop did for the first half-minute after he smelled smoke. I keep hoping to find a painting of this scene: Saint Martin, eyes wide with fright, desperately tugging with both hands at the rusty bolt as flames lick at his robe. That is a saint I could identify with.

I've experienced that minute of panic often enough, when I've forgotten that God is there with me. In the flames of difficult situations, when everything seems to be coming apart, I take too long to hand things over to the Lord. I, like Saint Martin, the great Bishop of Tours, have wasted time tugging at the rusty bolt and only later remembered to stop trying to control things and turn confidently to the power of prayer.

Maybe I could settle for a picture of the saint lying in prayer on the burning floor, untouched by the flames all around him. In any case, Martin of Tours is the one I pray to for the grace to keep my cool when I'm starting to panic. He knows what that feeling is like.

The blur of gray buildings is well behind us now, and the train continues rattling southwest toward the sea. No one else is looking out the window.

Reflection

One of the elder monks in the Egyptian desert once said, "It isn't because evil thoughts come to us that we are condemned, but only because we make use of evil thoughts. Of course, it can happen that we suffer shipwreck because of these thoughts, but it can also happen that because of them we are crowned." The lesson of Saint Martin's fire is that God sometimes asks us to pass through temptations or trying times for reasons we can't understand. Can you think of a time when you were beginning to panic, and then remembered to turn everything over to the Lord? Is there some trial in your life right now that may be an opportunity to turn to God in trusting prayer?

Sacred Scripture (Dan. 3:21–25, RSV)

Then these men were bound in their mantles, their tunics, their hats, and their other garments, and they were cast into the burning fiery furnace. Because the king's order was strict and the furnace very hot, the flame of the fire slew those men who took up Shadrach, Meshach, and Abednego. And these three men, Shadrach, Meshach, and Abednego, fell bound into the burning fiery furnace. Then King Nebuchadnezzar was astonished and rose up in haste. He said to his counselors, "Did we not cast three men bound into the fire?" They answered the king, "True, O king." He answered, "But I see four men loose, walking in the midst of the fire, and they are not hurt; and the appearance of the fourth is like a son of the gods."

Rule of Benedict (Chapter 7, "Humility," vv. 36–40)

Scripture has it, "Anyone who perseveres to the end will be saved," and again, "Be brave of heart and rely on the Lord." . . . [The faithful] are so confident in their expectation of reward from God that they continue joyfully and say, "But in all this we overcome because of him who so greatly loved us." Elsewhere Scripture says: "O God, you have tested us, you have tried us as silver is tried by fire."

Thursday of the Fifth Week of Lent

Chambord, France:
Gaining Perspective

My friend Jean and I are standing on the vast lawn that lies in front of the gigantic chateau of Chambord. The fertile farmland of the Loire Valley, an hour's ride south of Paris, was always considered worth fighting over. During the middle ages, fortified castles—*châteaux*—sprang up all along the valley as various nobles tried to defend their domains. With the coming of gunpowder and cannons and the end of feudal warfare, these forts lost their military value and were converted into fashionable residences. Elegant windows were cut into their walls and lovely flower gardens laid out in their moats. The chateaux built later were never fortresses at all, but were designed from the start as splendid country residences. The most outrageous example of the later kind of chateau is Chambord.

Even at this distance, well back from the building, it's hard to take in the whole thing in one glance. Its 365 chimneys and scores of spires and pinnacles float like an aerial village of gray slate above the imposing five-story façade. On this side alone, there seem to be enough windows for most of the 440 rooms. Built as a hunting lodge for King Francis the First, this triumph of playfulness and fantasy was the first flowering of the Renaissance in France.

We start to stroll around outside Chambord's imposing bulk in the afternoon sun, overwhelmed by its size and charmed by the variety of its architectural surprises. Jean stops in his tracks and breaks into a broad smile. "*Excusez, moi, père*, but I see an old friend over there from my army regiment. It's been so many years! Let me go and say hello. I'll be back in a minute."

The two are immediately lost in an animated conversation, and it's obvious that this will take more than a minute. I wander a discreet distance away from them to watch the activity on the front lawn. A large hot-air balloon, glowing white and blue in the sunshine, is just lifting off. It glides slowly upward like a mysterious vision, a giant soap bubble hovering silently over the spires of Chambord.

I think of little Kari, my friend's six-year-old back home, giving me a long account of her classroom birthday party. She told me that each child had been given a helium-filled balloon. I asked her, "What would happen if you let go of the string on your balloon?" She answered matter-of-factly, "Oh! It would fall up!"

As a creature held down by the heavy hand of gravity, I was fascinated at the time by the image of a thing dropping not toward the earth but toward the sky. There was something delightful about the notion of "falling up."

All Christians, and especially monks, are supposed to approach life with a certain lightness of spirit, not weighed down by worries or by what Benedict calls "too great concern for the fleeting and temporal things of this world." I don't always manage to live up to the ideal myself, though— my life can grow pretty heavy with worrying about my various jobs, projects, and deadlines. This afternoon, far away from my office, I find myself asking what would happen if I let go of the weight of all that worrying and lightened up in my approach to life. Maybe I'd fall up.

The hot-air balloonists rising gently over the fantastic chimneys and towers of Chambord could teach all of us some lessons in Christian spirituality. First, they have a sense of perspective. From their vantage point, they can see the whole chateau, its fifty-five-square-kilometer wooded estate and the farmland beyond. Balloonists have a sense of the real lay of the land. If I were to lighten up, maybe I'd be able to rise far enough above my tasks and my troubles to see them in their true proportions and not let them become more important than they really are.

Second, balloonists aren't preoccupied with the future; they don't know exactly where the wind is going to take them; they just savor the present moment. If I responded to deadlines and the pressures of planning with the tranquillity of the balloonist, I'd probably be easier to live with. But wouldn't I also be less effective? Less efficient? Somehow, as I watch the calm gracefulness of the blue balloon, the weighty words "effective" and "efficient" seem to lose their hold over me. I imagine myself up there with the balloonists floating high above the countryside, feeling the gentle breeze on my face, and smiling as I look down at the carefree play of pinnacles and gables on the chateau's roof below. I start to take in the view. . . .

Jean has finished his visit and is striding quickly down the path toward me with an apologetic look on his face. Time to bring myself gently back to earth. At least for now.

Reflection

Lent, like a long pilgrimage, is an opportunity to step back from your daily life and see it from a different perspective, the way a balloonist gains a new perspective from high overhead. You may begin to see more clearly, for example, how God takes care of you and sustains you, or how precious you are in the Lord's eyes despite your faults.

Think of a certain problem in your life and ask the Lord to give you a new perspective on it. Now think of someone or something that you value very much, and ask the Lord to let you see that person or thing in God's wider view.

Sacred Scripture (Matt. 6:25, 26, 34, RSV)

Therefore I tell you, do not be anxious about your life, what you shall eat or what you shall drink, nor about your body, what you shall put on. Is not life more than food, and the body more than clothing? Look at the birds of the air: they neither sow nor reap nor gather into barns, and yet your heavenly Father feeds them. Are you not of more value than they? Therefore do not be anxious about tomorrow, for tomorrow will be anxious for itself. Let the day's own trouble be sufficient for the day.

Wisdom of the Desert

"Abba Euprepios said, 'Knowing that God is faithful and mighty, have faith in him and you will share what is his. . . . As for your own affairs, believe with faith in him about them, too, for he is able to work miracles in you also.'"[5]

---

5. Benedicta Ward, ed., *Daily Readings with the Desert Fathers* (Springfield, IL: Templegate Publishers, 1990), 88.

Friday of the
Fifth Week of Lent

Amsterdam, Holland:
Hoping No Matter What

A young mother plods across the snow-covered bridge, tugging a tiny sled made entirely of wood. On it sits a rosy-cheeked child in a blue snowsuit, holding on with both mittens. I pick my way carefully along the narrow icy sidewalk that runs beside Amsterdam's Prinsegracht canal. The white cover of snow glistens in the January sun, a startling contrast to the jet black water.

In the seventeenth century, when Holland was one of the great commercial powers of the world, Amsterdam's merchants built the canals that give the city her unique character. On the narrow streets alongside each canal they built endless rows of stately brick houses that peer down into the water this afternoon.

In this particular neighborhood, the waterfront buildings are more modest, and some have small businesses on their ground floors. I arrive in front of number 263 Prinsegracht. At the time of the Nazi invasion of Holland, this was a factory and warehouse belonging to a Mr. Kugler, a dealer in spices. Two of his employees, Herman van Pels and Otto Frank, were Jews. During the worst days of the German occupation, when Jews were being hunted down and deported to death camps, Kugler let his two employees hide with their families in a secret set of rooms in the back of his warehouse.

Among the eight people in hiding was Frank's daughter, Anne, a bright and sensitive girl who had just turned thirteen when they entered the annex. During two years of hiding she kept a diary that was found and published after her death. This book, *The Diary of a Young Girl,* has touched the hearts of millions of readers throughout the world, and has made number 263 Prinsegracht into a grisly pilgrimage shrine.

There is nothing to distinguish the building from the others on the block: its narrow brick façade is taken up almost entirely by large windows that stare wide-eyed at the street and the canal. I stamp the snow off my boots and climb several steps into a very simple lobby where I pay the admission charge for a visit to "The Anne Frank House."

I follow a couple of other visitors up a narrow wooden stairway to the second floor. The old stairs protest noisily, creaking under our feet. On the landing at the top, I see the bookcase that swung on hinges to conceal the secret stairs leading to the hidden rooms in back. The first room beyond it, now bare of furniture, is the Franks' living room where Mr. and Mrs. Frank slept. Next to it is Anne's cubicle that she'd decorated with pictures of movie stars. Some of the yellowed clippings are still on the wall just as she describes them. Excerpts from her diary are posted in appropriate places in the different rooms. There has been no attempt to re-create the mood of the place with substitute furniture or sound effects. Nor is there any need to—the empty rooms are alive with the sad, courageous spirits of the frightened people who hid here for two years. Having read Anne's diary myself, I feel I know them all: Mr. and Mrs. Frank and their first daughter, Margot; Mr. and Mrs. Van Pels and their son, sixteen-year-old Peter; and Fritz Pfeffer.

The spirit of the owner, Mr. Kugler, is here, too, along with those of his employees Miep and Jan Gies and other selfless people who risked their own lives every day for two years to support the eight fugitives, bringing them food and supplies, local news, and much-needed encouragement.

The person whose presence I sense most of all, of course, is Anne—sensitive, passionate, insightful, courageous, and optimistic. The recent complete and unexpurgated edition of her diary shows her to be, in addition, a headstrong and self-centered teenager given to normal outbursts of immaturity and moodiness. She had hoped to be a writer someday.

As I climb the steps to the top floor that doubled as the kitchen and as the Van Pels' bedroom, I start to sense another presence in these rooms, something both subtle and overwhelming at the same time. It is the sinister sense of evil that floats through the whole place like some poisonous haze. Anne Frank's hideout is crowded with millions of ghosts: not only the Jews of the Holocaust, but every victim of Central American death squads, every American Black lynched by Klansmen in the middle of the night, every political prisoner ever kidnapped and tortured, every woman and child victim of genocide in Rwanda and the former Yugoslavia. . . .

Downstairs, fists begin pounding on the secret door—the one hidden behind the bookcase. Rifle butts and Gestapo boots crash through the thin wood and into the hiding place. It is August 4, 1944. All eight of the occupants are quickly dragged off to concentration camps at Auschwitz or Bergen-Belsen. The young girl's diaries are left scattered on the floor.

Miep Gies will gather them up the next day and put them away for safe-keeping, unread.

Anne Frank will die in Bergen-Belsen, three months short of her six-teenth birthday, just weeks before the Allies arrive to liberate the camp. Her mother and sister will die, too. Only Otto Frank will survive.

Weighed down with pessimism about the future of humanity, I force myself to keep moving through the last tiny room and follow the tour arrows down some narrow stairs. In the small ground-floor museum, there are several displays about present-day racism and political repres-sion. Large placards hold quotations from Anne's diary. One of them seems particularly poignant under the circumstances:

> In spite of everything, I still believe that people are really good at heart. If I look up to the heavens, I think that this will all come right, that this cruelty too will end, and that peace and tranquillity will return again.

I'm not sure whether to be uplifted by Anne's courageous spirit or depressed by the power of the hatred that killed her. Finally depression wins—I've had about all the hatred and killing I can take for one day.

As I step outside, the cold, damp wind rushing across the Prinsegracht bites into my cheeks. I wrap my scarf over my mouth and nose and set off through the frozen streets with a heavy heart. Soon I'm back in the crowded center of town where streetcars and bicycles spatter through the slush in the cloudy gray afternoon. Squat, sturdy boats rumble mourn-fully about their business on the icy ink of the Heerengracht canal.

I'm snapped out of my gloomy thoughts by an unexpected splash of color off to my left. A poster-sized photograph is sparkling in the window of a bus tour agency: bright yellow tulips stretch endlessly across a field beneath a clear blue sky. Alongside the picture are the dates and prices for the spring tours of tulip fields that are still buried in snow this afternoon. I step closer to the plate glass window for a better look. It's a lovely pic-ture: acres of tulips glowing in the warm spring sunshine, inviting me to come and join them.

I stand still for a few moments trying to put myself into the photo-graph. I try to feel the warm breeze on my face and the sun on my back. I try to smell the rich aroma of the moist, fertile soil and touch the velvet petals. But it doesn't work—this is just not tulip season.

Sometimes Jesus expects to meet me in the pain of a difficult or depressing situation, so I better show up there to meet him. The cross is, after all, our unique way into the mysterious suffering heart of God. Well, this afternoon, the Lord of Love is obviously not looking for me in that meadow of Easter flowers, but on this slushy sidewalk. The voice of the One who died and rose is speaking to me not from the glorious empty tomb, but from the ominous empty rooms of the Anne Frank House.

My hands are getting cold even inside my gloves, so I clap them together a few times to help the circulation as I turn wistfully from the tulip field. I continue crunching my way carefully down the icy sidewalk.

Reflection

Our earthly pilgrimage, like Jesus', includes suffering and even death, but our faith assures us that human suffering, far from being an absurd accident, is somehow an integral part of our own story, just as it was of Christ's. What is your own experience of the mystery of suffering? Do you find that it brings you closer to God, or does it just push you farther away? Ask the Lord to give you the sense of confidence in God that Jesus had as he made his way up to Jerusalem.

Sacred Scripture (Isa. 50:5–8, RSV)

The Lord GOD has opened my ear, and I was not rebellious, I turned not backward. I gave my back to the smiters, and my cheeks to those who pulled out the beard; I hid not my face from shame and spitting. For the Lord GOD helps me; therefore I have not been confounded; therefore I have set my face like a flint, and I know that I shall not be put to shame; he who vindicates me is near.

Rule of Benedict (Chapter 7, "Humility," vv. 35–36)

"The fourth step of humility is that in this obedience under difficult, unfavorable, or even unjust conditions, his heart quietly embraces suffering, and endures it without weakening or seeking escape."

Saturday of the Fifth Week of Lent

Saint Gervais, Paris: Expecting Help

The Church of Saints Gervais et Protase stands in the Marais, one of the oldest neighborhoods in Paris. The first church that stood on this spot was a favorite of Saint Germain, Bishop of Paris about the year 550. King Louis XIII laid the foundation stone for the present building in 1616. This is the first time I've been inside, so, without being too obvious, I steal a peek at the great gothic church while waiting for Midday Prayer to begin. My eyes trace the lines of the great gray pillars that shoot out of the stone floor and zoom straight skyward into the shadows, where they curve gently until they join one another in a riot of points and arches far overhead.

Rue du Grenier sur l'eau Paris.

Kneeling on the floor of the large chapel located behind the main altar, I feel conspicuous in my black habit—the others around me are wearing white choir robes. Even more unusual is the fact that half of these people are women. I'm a guest of the "Community of Jerusalem," a monastic group founded in Paris in the 1970s to witness to God's presence in the center of the city.

My mind wanders to a wedding held here almost 400 years ago. The groom was Monsieur Antoine le Gras, and the bride was Mademoiselle Louise de Marillac. Catholics would one day come to know her as Saint Louise de Marillac.

Louise had a difficult life. As the "natural daughter" of Louis de Marillac and some unknown woman, she was painfully conscious of the dubious circumstances of her birth, and was not in line to inherit anything of the Marillac estate. Her father nevertheless saw to her upbringing and education.

Her marriage to Antoine Le Gras, a young man with a bright future at the royal court, finally seemed to promise some happiness. Shortly after the marriage, however, a political assassination and the disgrace of Le Gras' friend, Queen Marie de Medici, sent his political fortunes tumbling. Not long after this he fell gravely ill, and after suffering for five years, died in 1626, leaving Louise to care for their young son, Michel, who was to prove a very troubled and difficult child. She began to suffer from stomach problems that would beset her for the rest of her life. Louise de Marillac continued to struggle through years that gave her little joy and plenty of sadness.

A bell rings, and we all stand to sing the traditional opening words of the Church's Liturgy of the Hours "*Dieu, viens à mon aide! Seigneur, à notre secours!*" "O God, come to my assistance, O Lord, make haste to help us!" Then we sit down to sing the first psalm.

Around the time of her husband's death, Louise was introduced to her new spiritual director, a rough, cold, worn-looking priest from the provinces. Since he lacked the aristocratic polish and sophistication that Louise had come to expect from the Parisian clergy, Vincent de Paul made a poor first impression. But before long the saintly priest's wise counsel and encouragement began to profoundly change her life. The bond of friendship and cooperation that the two of them formed would benefit thousands, even millions of people over the coming centuries.

By having her organize and oversee his small group of pious women engaged in charitable works, Monsieur Vincent gave Louise an outlet for her deep-felt desire to serve the poor. Very soon, however, both of them recognized that the frightful poverty found everywhere in France was not going to be effectively addressed simply by occasional help from rich women volunteering a few hours a week. What was needed was women who would give not just alms or their spare time but their lives.

Thus Vincent and Louise came up with an innovative idea: a society of religious women who would not live behind cloister walls, but who would be dedicated to actively ministering to the poor and the sick wherever they were to be found. Their idea for *les Filles de la Charité*, the Daughters of Charity, would become the basic model for the rest of the church's active religious orders in the future.

Vincent de Paul has become one of the better-known Catholic saints, and usually gets the credit for the great success of the Daughters of Charity. But he would never have accomplished what he did if it were not for Louise de Marillac. She had always shown a talent for organization and administration, and as Vincent and Louise began to found their order, she showed many other gifts as well: in helping to write the "Rule" for the new order she combined a deep and solid spirituality with a sense for practical detail. She also proved to be an excellent teacher of the spiritual life as she helped train new the sisters, many of whom were simple girls from the countryside.

We chant another psalm, this one set to a melody with a Byzantine feel.

Their early efforts to help the poor were made more difficult by the years of severe economic disruption and moral and social turmoil caused by the political rebellion in France known as the Fronde. One of the works closest to Louise's heart at the time—the care of *enfants trouvés*, abandoned babies—became a particularly troublesome burden. With more and more helpless infants to care for, and with fewer and fewer economic resources to work with, the task soon went from daunting to overwhelming. When the civil government totally collapsed, it seemed to Louise that she might have to completely give up the whole effort. She wrote to Vincent: "I stand in very great need of the particular assistance of God at this time, for wherever I turn, and whatever I put my hand to, I see nothing but misery and affliction. . . ."

Eventually the "particular assistance of God" came when the government stepped in and took on the economic burden of caring for the foundlings, and the work could now proceed on a firm footing. Over the ensuing years the Daughters of Charity and the Vincentian order of men would continue to ease the misery of poor and needy people around the world, as they still do today.

We finish a final psalm and everyone kneels for a moment of silent prayer.

Perhaps the most endearing thing about Louise is that she accomplished so much despite a life filled with so much adversity. Although her life was filled with sadness, Louise not only survived, but was able to create with Saint Vincent de Paul an order of women religious that changed the face of Europe.

We stand, and the service comes to an end with an oration. As we file quietly out of the chapel and into the main body of the church, some of the sisters and brothers whisper warm greetings to various people who are waiting for a word with them.

I walk through the rear door and out into the sunlight. After crossing the busy street behind the church, I head down the quiet cobblestones of the charming and picturesque rue du Grenier sur l'Eau. These ancient buildings on either side of me, I realize, once looked down on the turmoil of la Fronde. Undoubtedly, too, they caught an occasional glimpse of Louise de Marillac hurrying by on her way to serve Christ in the poor or to deal with some business of Daughters of Charity, and counting all the time on God alone to keep her going.

Reflection

The Scripture readings assigned for the final weeks of Lent show Jesus becoming more and more aware of the deadly plot against him, and trusting more and more in the Lord. Louise lives out this trust under conditions that we can probably relate to more easily. Think of a time when serious difficulties piled up in your own life. What did that feel like? Did you sense that God was particularly distant at the time, or nearby? Did you experience God's help? If so, did you have to wait long for it?

Ask the Lord to help you imitate Saint Louise's confidence in God, especially at moments of pain or discouragement.

Sacred Scripture (Phil. 4:13, RSV)

"I can do all things in him who strengthens me."

Rule of Benedict (Chapter 7, "Humility," vv. 35–39)

The fourth step of humility is that in this obedience under difficult, unfavorable, or even unjust conditions, his heart quietly embraces suffering and endures it without weakening or seeking escape. For Scripture has it: "Anyone who perseveres to the end will be saved," and again, "Be brave of heart and rely on the Lord." Another passage shows how the faithful must endure everything, even contradiction, for the Lord's sake, saying in the person of those who suffer, "For your sake we are put to death continually; we are regarded as sheep marked for slaughter." They are so confident in their expectation of reward from God that they continue joyfully and say, "But in all this we overcome because of him who so greatly loved us."

HOLY WEEK

Arriving in Jerusalem

The escape through the Red Sea, the covenant at Sinai, and the forty years of desert wandering transformed a ragged band of sheep-herders into a holy nation, the People of God. The experience changed them forever.

Our meditations for this final week stress that our Lenten journey is not just a forty-day exercise after which we return to old ways. It is meant to change us permanently. The meditations for Monday and Wednesday, "Salamanca" and "Perpignan," both reflect the theme of transformation in Christ, while "Santa Cruz" shows how certain experiences have the power to change our hearts. "El Bosque" helps us learn from an eloquent ritual used in the Holy Thursday liturgy, while "Fatima Parish" challenges us with an unsettling variation of an ancient Good Friday ceremony. Finally, on Holy Saturday, "Saint Martin du Canigou" invites us to reflect on the goal of our journey: total transformation in and with the risen Lord.

Monday of Holy Week

Salamanca, Spain: Being Transformed

Salamanca, in northwest central Spain, has been staring down at the River Tormes since the time of the Caesars. Walking on the narrow railroad bridge high over the river, I keep glancing across at the two beautiful cathedrals that stand out against the gray February sky. The winter wind numbs my fingertips as I flip through my stack of homemade vocabulary cards on the way to Spanish class.

From here I can also see a couple of majestic convents lower down on the hillside. Both of these, like all of the town's palaces, churches, and university buildings, are made from the same local sandstone; Salamanca looks as if it's been hewn from a single huge honey-brown block.

At the end of the bridge I turn to my left, spread my arms wide for balance, and slide on tiptoe down the steep embankment, following a well-worn dirt path. I cut across the empty parking lot behind the police station, still studying my flashcards.

La Clerecía – Salamanca

Besides hardening with age and weathering into a variety of lovely tans and reddish golds, the local stone has one special feature: it's perfect for carving. Medieval sculptors working with it could actually imitate the intricate designs used on plates and medallions by Salamanca's silversmiths. Thus the name given to this kind of stone decoration: "*plateresco*," from the Spanish word for silver, *plata*.

I walk alongside the imposing bulk of the Dominican friars' *Convento de*

151

San Esteban, then past the graceful little gothic monastery of "*las Duenas*" belonging to the Sisters of Saint James, and turn left into a narrow alley that slices straight up the steep hill toward the university.

The University of Salamanca was founded in 1200 as Spain's first university, and soon made the town the most respected center of learning in all of Europe. Her narrow, almost treeless streets still bustle with clusters of students on their way to class in buildings 600 years old.

At the top of the hill, shoppers, students, and tourists come and go on the sidewalks in the calm, measured rhythm of any small Spanish town. I check my watch. Good! I still have a few minutes before class, enough time to pay a visit to one of the town's favorite attractions—the frog. I stroll up a street lined with souvenir shops and jewelry stores. There are frogs in every shop window—frogs of silver, frogs of gold, frogs in china, plaster, and plastic. There are frog T-shirts, frog coffee mugs, and frog ashtrays.

I turn a corner and in a minute I'm standing in front of the main building of the University of Salamanca. Its ornate façade, made up of carved stone panels towering three stories above the twin wooden doors, is one of the masterpieces of plateresque carving. Commissioned by Ferdinand and Isabella in the late 1520s, it is crowded with floral motifs, royal portraits, characters from pagan mythology, and secret symbols.

Scholars disagree on the exact identity of many of the figures: is that Isabel of Portugal or is it the goddess Hebe? Is that couple in the upper right corner Eve and Cain or Venus and Mars? In any case, it seems likely that many of the figures tell the story of the painful process by which a student in the middle ages would, by dint of long, hard work, pass through various stages and long years of study until he finally reached his goal and became a doctor of law or philosophy.

You can easily pick out Hercules, for example, in his lion-skin disguise, holding a club. He's there to remind the students that university studies are as difficult as the twelve labors of Hercules.

Several young men with textbooks under their arms pass beneath the façade. Embroiled in their own lively discussion, they're oblivious to the equally animated conversation going on above their heads among mythical heroes, monarchs, prelates, and demigods.

The most beloved of all those carved figures is almost hidden down in the lower right-hand corner: a little stone frog, known as *la rana buena suerte*, "the frog of good luck," is Salamanca's unofficial mascot. Squatting there on top of a human skull, however, it is not a sign of good luck at all, nor a symbol of gradual success or hard work. This tiny creature is one of the most powerful symbols on the whole façade. It's a symbol of *transformation*.

Transformation is the central driving force in the world of living things, yet it is so common that we take it for granted. We're used to the idea that seeds become flowers, caterpillars turn into butterflies, and acorns become oak trees. As common as this process is, however, it remains one of the great mysteries of nature: a creature actually stops being one thing in order to become something else.

No one thinks of a flower as just a big seed, or an oak tree as simply an overgrown acorn. A flower happens only because some seed stops being a seed. An oak tree happens only when some acorn, buried in the cold, dark earth, stops being an acorn, bursts open, and becomes something new.

This, then, is the symbolism of *la rana*. A frog begins life as something else, a tadpole. The purpose of a tadpole is to stop being a tadpole one day in order to become a frog. A tadpole whose life's goal was to become the biggest, fattest, shiniest tadpole in the world would be missing the whole reason for being a tadpole in the first place—and would probably end up a very unhappy little creature. The tadpole has to die to its wiggling tail and sleek shape so that a new frog can come into the pond.

A chilly gust of wind rushes into the stony little plaza, twists itself into invisible tangles, and charges out the far end. I dig my cold hands further into my jacket pockets; my fingers close around my pack of vocabulary cards. Oops! Better check my watch again . . . time to head to class.

Jesus uses an image of transformation to teach one of his central ideas: "Unless the grain of wheat falls to the earth and dies, it remains just a grain of wheat." What's true of seeds, acorns, and tadpoles, he is saying, is true of me as well. Jesus never challenges me to be a better Christian, never asks me to improve, to become holier or more saintly. He never asks me to grow. He simply keeps asking me to be transformed—to die.

It's clear enough that a caterpillar is meant to be transformed into a butterfly, and a tadpole into a frog. But what kind of being am *I* supposed to be transformed into? Saint Basil of Caesaria answers boldly: "A human being is a creature whose purpose is to become God." Saint Paul announces the same thing to the Galatians, "It is no longer I who live, but it is Christ who lives in me."

In order to be transformed into a new being, however, I have to follow Jesus' example, and do what he did on the cross: let go of everything I am, everything I have, everything I'm familiar with. If I try to hold onto the comfortable predictability of gradual growth, I'll be like the tadpole who just wants to be a bigger tadpole, and my life will have no real purpose. I can become Christ only in the dozens of daily deaths I die to my old self: when I reach out in love to someone at the risk of being rejected or hurt, or when I gamble everything in deep, self-abandoning prayer, or when I surrender to God's will for me in some disagreeable task.

This is why the monastic vows ceremony is modeled on the baptismal rite—complete with the clothing in a new garment and the praying of the litany of the saints—to remind the candidates that they are leaving behind an old life to take up a new and different one. We become who we really are only when we let go of the security and safety of the known and allow the Spirit to make something entirely new out of us.

Another group of university students saunters past me speaking American English. As I turn to follow them to class, I nod *adios* to Ferdinand and Isabella, Hercules and Hera, and, of course, the frog.

Reflection

Lent is still used as a time to prepare adults for baptism, the sacrament in which we are buried with Christ in the saving waters so as to rise with him to a new life. Since all of us are continually being called to be transformed into Christ, Lent is the perfect time to discover things that are holding us back: old grudges and resentments for example. Think of something that you need to "die to," and ask the Lord to help you to let go of it so that you may be better prepared for the transforming event of Easter.

Sacred Scripture (John 12:24, RSV)

"Truly, truly, I say to you, unless a grain of wheat falls into the earth and dies, it remains alone; but if it dies, it bears much fruit."

Rule of Benedict (Prologue, v. 3)

"This message of mine is for you, then, if you are ready to give up your own will, once and for all."

Tuesday of
Holy Week

Santa Cruz, Bolivia:
Feeling Christ Suffer

She is barefoot, wearing the common dress of Bolivian Indian women, with underskirts that puff out to make her look unnaturally heavy in the hips. Her jet black braids disappear over her shoulders and down her back. The young mother is just greeting us when her husband comes trotting up from somewhere across the dusty lot to join the group. Their house, really just a shed, is one of several strewn about among the low tropical shrubs and scrawny trees. It's a slab of concrete with wooden walls and a corrugated metal roof. The couple lead Father Jim, Sister Ana, and me solemnly into their tiny home.

The single room has windows only in the front wall next to the door, so that even on this mild autumn day in May, it's hot inside. Two twin beds shoved together take up half of the entire place. The family's belongings fit onto a few shelves next to the wheelbarrow that's leaning against a wall. There's no plumbing to be seen. No stove. Their three-year-old daughter, whom I've been carrying, squirms out of my arms and runs off past her parents and out the door. Her dirty white dress is the same one she had on at the 7 o'clock Mass last night when I was concelebrating with Father Joe, an English diocesan priest newly arrived in Bolivia. . . .

It was time for the "Sign of Peace," and the two of us walked out into the wide airy nave to exchange a handshake and a greeting with the seventy-five or so people. It was also a chance to bless the little babies and make a fuss over the toddlers. Toward the rear of the church stood a dark-skinned Indian couple, their dress and their faces gave them away as simple country people, *campesinos*. I'd noticed them filing in late, the mother sober and preoccupied, the little girl in the white dress, and the father carrying the baby wrapped in a white blanket. When I came up to him he carefully switched his precious bundle to his other arm and shook my hand. To see the infant, I slowly lifted back a corner of the baby blanket, noticing the pattern of flowers—little pink and blue ones. A shiny dark eye sparkled up at me. I gently touched the baby's cheek with the knuckle of my first finger. Then as I lifted my hand in a blessing, an old woman's voice rasped in a loud stage whisper "*Está muerte, padre. Tiene que baptisarlo.*" My hand stopped in mid-blessing, as the words hit home, "He's dead, Father. You have to baptize him." I stared down at the tiny face again and realized to my horror that the glistening eye was in fact not moving or blinking. It was frozen there like a bead of black glass. I felt as if the earth had just gaped open under my feet. In a daze, I mechanically replaced the corner of the blanket over the dead baby's face and told the parents to wait until after Mass. I returned to the altar in a stunned trance. . . .

To the left of the twin beds, on a table, lies a small white casket, closed tight. A couple of neighbors have now squeezed into the small room to pray with the heartbroken parents whose faces are haggard with grief and shock. Father Jim, Sister Ana, and I have come to celebrate the "funeral," a simple prayer service at home before the body is taken to the cemetery.

The priest sprinkles holy water and says an opening prayer in the stuffy room. As Sister begins a Scripture reading, I watch the mother standing near me. The sharp, almost craggy features of her young face are contorted in pain. That's the way she looked last night when they brought the dead baby straight from the hospital to Mass to ask us to baptize him. . . .

In the back pews of church after the Mass, a group of curious onlookers joined the family and friends in the impromptu prayers for the baby. Father Joe explained that the child didn't need to be baptized, that he was already with God, but that we could pray together and give him a blessing.

"*¿Como se llama?*" he asked gently, "What is the baby's name?"

"*Se llama Juan Domingo,*" the mother whispered, "His name is Juan Domingo." Then she began to pour out her tragic story to the sympathetic ear of Father Joe.

Just this morning, a newspaper article had given some grim statistics about the quality of life in the Bolivian state of Santa Cruz. As Juan Domingo's mother told her tragic story in a soft, half-choking voice, the newspaper's cold statements and abstract numbers seemed to answer her like the mocking chorus of a Greek tragedy.

"My baby had terrible diarrhea." "*The most common cause of death in children in Latin America is dehydration due to simple diarrhea.*"

"We had no doctor to go to, but finally we brought him in to the hospital in town." "*Thirty-four percent have no health services available to them.*"

"The first thing the doctor said to me when he looked at my son was 'This baby is dirty!'" "*Forty-five percent have no running water, but rely on wells, pumps, and tanks.*"

"When I told him that my son had very bad diarrhea, the doctor scolded me. He shouted, 'Why do you feed your children water that has not been boiled first?'" "*Forty-seven percent lack access to basic sanitation.*"

"He died in the hospital soon after we brought him there. My little son! My little son!" Now the response had an American accent: "*Well, in third world countries life is cheap; babies there are always dying, so people are used to it.*" Someone, I thought to myself, ought to come and tell this mother that she's supposed to be used to it. She looks as heartbroken as any grieving mother I've ever seen in the United States. . . .

It's very still in here. You can hear the flies buzzing during the reading and the short homily. There's a litany, some final prayers for the devastated parents, then a parting blessing for baby Juan Domingo in his little white casket.

We step outside into the cool fresh air, and the parents thank us for coming; to have two priests and a sister at Juan Domingo's funeral was a great honor.

The three of us whisper sympathetic good-byes and leave the family and the silent neighbors to their tears. We climb into our rugged vehicle for the bone-jarring ride back along the dirt track.

Soon my weeks in Bolivia will be over and I'll be back in my monastery in the United States. The reality of the "third world" will probably fade into a vague memory, a series of interesting color snapshots in an album. I'll still feel as helpless as ever in the face of so much poverty and suffering in the world. Especially when I start teaching school.

"*Forty-eight percent of the population will never have a chance to go to school.*" Last night's Greek chorus of statistics interrupts my musings once again. Suddenly I realize that something has happened to me in the past twenty-four hours, something that has changed me forever. Now the statistics speak with a human voice—the haunting whisper of a heartbroken mother with black braids. Now the numbers have a face—a little brown one with a single black glassy eye staring up at me. Today, third world statistics have been given a name—Juan Domingo.

I am richer and more sensitive for having met him. Now Juan Domingo sleeps forever in my heart, cradled in his father's arms and wrapped in a white baby blanket with flowers on it—little pink and blue ones.

Reflection

One important dimension of the gospel's call to conversion is "social justice." Lent's discipline of fasting and almsgiving should make us more conscious of our egoism as individuals and as a nation.

As you read the parable of the rich man and Lazarus below, notice that the poor man has a name, Lazarus. No character in any other parable has a name. Think about what Jesus might be trying to tell us by giving the beggar a name. Ask yourself if needy people are very "real" for you. Do you let yourself be touched by the plight of those who you see every day? Or do you treat them the way the rich man treated Lazarus, perhaps not even noticing their existence? What is your attitude toward the millions of poor and starving people around the world? What do you think Jesus expects of you?

Sacred Scripture (Luke 16:19–23, RSV)

There was a rich man, who was clothed in purple and fine linen and who feasted sumptuously every day. And at his gate lay a poor man named Lazarus, full of sores, who desired to be fed with what fell from the rich man's table; moreover the dogs came and licked his sores. The poor man died and was carried by the angels to Abraham's bosom. The rich man also died and was buried; and in Hades, being in torment, he lifted up his eyes, and saw Abraham far off and Lazarus in his bosom. . . .

Rule of Benedict
(Chapter 4, "The Tools for Good Works," vv. 14–19)

"You must relieve the lot of the poor, clothe the naked, visit the sick and bury the dead."

Wednesday of Holy Week

Perpignan, France: Dancing with God

The evening is perfect for a stroll around the old quarter of Perpignan, the central city of Catalonia in France. Catalonia, which spans the eastern end of the Pyrenees from Perpignan down to Barcelona in Spain, has a strong ethnic identity based on its rich cultural heritage, proud history, and common language, Catalan.

I can see, about a block ahead, cafe tables crowded together into a semicircle under their bright blue umbrellas. They form the curved side of a large, open plaza. Along its straight side runs the high wall of a grumpy old fortress called the Castillet. Against this old stone building, a

temporary platform has been set up with two rows of chairs on it.

As I arrive in the plaza I pass a wooden sign hanging on the wall of the Castillet: "*Sardane ce soir 20:00 h.*"— tonight they're going to dance the sardana, the traditional folk dance of Catalonia, here at eight o'clock. A crowd has already started to gather and a couple of men are sitting up on the platform holding trumpets. I smile at my good luck—I've arrived just in time.

Suddenly, floodlights pour a golden glow onto the Castillet and the sense of expectation grows as people begin to line the edges of the plaza. Twenty musicians in white open-necked shirts and black pants

159

or skirts are warming up. There are clarinet-like woodwinds, trumpets, a bass violin, and a piccolo.

The band launches into a pleasant, lively folk melody. Everyone listens appreciatively. A young woman, obviously the leader of the musicians, sets the tempo on a tiny drum the size and shape of a rolled up newspaper. Another warm-up tune is followed by a minute or two of rest. Then the leader gives three smart whacks on her drum: *tock! tock! tock!* The musicians begin a leisurely, lilting air that is different from the first two. A few people leave their cafe tables and walk slowly out into the empty center of the cobblestone plaza. A couple from a different table joins them, and then another, until there are about twenty people holding hands in a circle. They start dancing the sardana, with hands held motionless at shoulder height, each dancer clasping the hand of the person on either side, men alternating with women. The circle doesn't rotate—everyone stays in place as their feet weave what seems to me an intricate set of steps. There are young people in the circle, but they're far outnumbered by those in their fifties and older. The tempo is very slow and relaxed. Then the beat starts to increase and the dancers' light feet begin speeding up to keep pace until the final crescendo when the dance comes to a sudden end. Everyone applauds as the dancers drift slowly back to their coffee cups and wine glasses. The musicians play another folk tune and then pause for a short rest.

Tock! tock! tock! The leader's drum starts the band off again in a slow, swinging sardana gait. This time a few dozen people leave their chairs and come out into the plaza, spontaneously forming three circles, then four. Each group joins hands to make a motionless wreath of arms and shoulders that bobs slightly while feet draw deft, noiseless patterns on the paving stones.

In the wall of the Castillet, just above the gateway, is a niche containing a statue. A stone Virgin Mary, holding her baby, is looking down on the dance. I remember a medieval song called "My Dancing Day" in which Jesus, the leader of the dance, calls us all to join him:

> In a manger laid and wrapped I was
> So very poor this was my chance
> Betwixt an ox and a silly old ass,
> To call my true love to the dance . . .

These sardana dancers seem proud of what they are doing. "This," they are saying to the watching tourists, "this is us! We are proud of being Catalonians." Another verse of the song comes to mind:

Before Pilate then was I brought
Where Barabbas had deliverance;
They scourged me and set me at naught,
Judged me to die to lead the dance . . .

There is a beautiful unity in a sardana circle: old people and young, men and women, in dresses and in jeans. A pony-tailed man holds the hand of an older woman in a long skirt and a lovely silk blouse. These two may have never met before, but here in the circle they are mysteriously united, sharing the same elegant steps. As I watch this scene, the last verse of the song comes to me. Jesus sings:

Then up to heaven I did ascend
Where now I dwell in sure substance,
On the right hand of God, that all
May come unto the general dance . . .

All at once, I imagine the four circles becoming one big one. Chinese people in subdued gray outfits are pouring out of the side streets to join the dance, along with Nigerian women in bright-colored head-wraps. The circle starts getting larger and larger as South Americans with faces like Inca carvings stream onto the plaza to join with little children from Iraq and Israel, all holding hands in the one big sardana.

The circle has now reached far beyond the plaza, past the canal, and down across the river Têt. My brothers from the monastery arrive in their black habits to join Buddhist monks and Eskimos; there are Bosnians, Serbs, and Croats and Australian aborigines. And still they keep pouring in to join the dance. Protestants from Belfast arrive to clasp hands in the circle with their Catholic neighbors. The line stretches out of sight now in both directions. Everyone is dancing to the music with chins held high, as if to say, "This is us! We are one proud people!"

I jump up from my table and join the dance with my brothers and sisters in this single enormous sardana. My eyes fill with tears: I am holding hands with the whole world! A voice from inside says to me, "Yes! This is the way it could be. The way it *would* be if we were to let the Lord lead the dance." Then, to my amazement, my parents and grandparents who died years ago are there, too, hands held elegantly, their feet effortlessly going through the steps. The pace increases, and feet tap faster and faster. The ground itself is vibrating with the rhythm. This is the final crescendo. . . .

Suddenly I'm back in reality. Everyone is applauding, and the dancers are drifting back once more to their coffee cups and wine glasses. The cobblestones are empty as the band strikes up another interlude. It's time for me to leave to catch the midnight train for Rome. I stand and start off, alone once again, on the one-mile walk to the station. There is a light sardana bounce to my step.

An ancient monastic tradition holds that the monastery foreshadows the kingdom of heaven by the way the monks live together in unity, with no one seeking his own will, no one competing with another, but each trying to help his brother.

Well, even in the holiest monastery we still have a long way to go. And so does the rest of the world. But every now and then we catch a little glimpse of the General Dance. Every time someone acts like a brother or sister to someone else, the world draws a step closer to its goal of unity. A little white child walks to school holding hands with her African American classmate. The Christians in a certain town put Chanukah lights in their windows as a sign of solidarity with a Jewish family victimized by anti-Semitic vandalism. Two warring factions in some troubled country agree to stop fighting and open peace negotiations. Each of these is a preview of what is surely going to happen one day sooner or later.

On that day, the Lord of the Dance, Jesus himself, will appear seated on a throne in shining majesty and will invite all the peoples of the world to join hands as sisters and brothers. One great circle of humanity will stretch across the entire globe and reach upward into the clouds of heaven. The Lord will stand up, and the whole universe will fall silent, holding its breath in expectation.

Then he will give the signal to start the General Dance—three smart raps on a little drum: *tock! tock! tock!*

Reflection

The image of the crucified Jesus leading the dance suggests that his suffering gives meaning to our own pain and affliction, making them part of a mysterious pattern, part of the dance. Think of a time when the crucified Savior has asked you to follow him in the dance by sharing his pain and suffering. What was your response to his invitation?

During this Holy Week ask Jesus to help you respond more willingly to his call as Lord of the Dance.

Sacred Scripture (Rev. 21:1–5)

"Then I saw a new heaven and a new earth; for the first heaven and the first earth had passed away, and the sea was no more. And I saw the holy city, new Jerusalem, coming down out of heaven from God, prepared as a bride adorned for her husband. . . . And the one who was seated upon the throne said, 'See, I am making all things new.'"

Rule of Benedict
(Chapter 72, "The Good Zeal of Monks," vv. 11–12)

"Let them prefer nothing whatever to Christ, and may he bring us all together to everlasting life."

Holy Thursday

El Bosque, Bolivia:
Washing Feet

Night is falling fast on the outskirts of Santa Cruz, Bolivia. Our taxi turns off the busy main road and starts to bounce past patches of semitropical woods where cinder block shacks huddle together in groups as if looking for moral support. In the front seat, next to the driver, sits Gertulio, a Brazilian catechist. I'm in the back with a seminarian named Carlos who has volunteered to come out here and help me celebrate the Holy Thursday Mass. I've never been the chief celebrant on Holy Thursday—but at least I have said Mass in Spanish three times before.

We jolt to a stop at the edge of a wide, dark field. Mass kit in hand, I climb out of the cab and tramp through the high grass, the taxi's headlights throwing long eerie shadows in front of me. Forty yards ahead, the mission chapel of El Bosque is aglow with fluorescent lights. Sister Ana and Sister Teresa, two Bolivian sisters who live and work in El Bosque, greet us at the wide doorway. I can see over their shoulders into the single large room with a bare concrete floor. A portable altar and long wooden benches have been set up for Mass, and about two dozen people are already waiting patiently for the service to start. A couple of friendly dogs wander among the benches, but no one pays any attention to them. Carlos starts to unpack the Mass articles while I go sit on a bench in a far corner to hear confessions.

After twenty minutes the benches are full, and I walk over to say hi to the music ministers, several teenagers using an electric keyboard, a drum, and a few guitars. Then I vest for Mass.

The Holy Thursday Eucharist begins with loud, heartfelt, joyful singing. Soon it's time for me to read the gospel. Today's passage is from the thirteenth chapter of Saint John, in which Jesus washes the disciples' feet at the Last Supper, telling them, "If I then, your Lord and Teacher, have washed your feet, you also ought to wash one another's feet. For I have

given you an example, that you also should do as I have done to you."
Later in the Mass I will perform the Holy Thursday rite of footwashing, in
which the presiding priest dramatizes the gospel story of Jesus' action at
the Last Supper by washing the feet of twelve people from the congregation who represent the apostles.

The earliest Christians used footwashing as a ritual for welcoming guests into their homes, and included it in the first baptismal rite.
Caesarius of Arles, a sixth-century bishop, said in a Holy Thursday sermon how sad and disappointed he was to see Christians abandoning the
custom of washing one another's feet.

I finish reading the gospel and sit down as Sister Ana begins a lovely
reflection on the meaning of Holy Thursday and Jesus' message of love.

At about the same time that Bishop Caesarius was lamenting the death
of the Christian custom of footwashing, Saint Benedict was preserving it
for future generations in his *Rule*. In Chapter 35 he calls for the weekly
table servers to wash the feet of all the monks, and in Chapter 53 he orders
the abbot and the brethren to wash the feet of the monastery's guests.
Thus the ritual of footwashing would be kept alive for several centuries
by the monks.

During the middle ages, the Benedictines continued washing each
other's feet, but not those of their guests. The latter custom was replaced
by a new one—the washing of the feet of poor people. Under the influence of this example, Christian kings and nobles began performing this
ritual gesture toward the poor once a year. Some medieval abbeys celebrated Holy Thursday with as many as three different footwashing rites.

Sister Ana has finished her biblical reflection. Long wooden benches
are set out in a straight line in front of the altar, and the people who
have been designated begin coming up to have the priest wash their feet.
I remove my white chasuble, and dressed simply in my long white alb
and stole, walk over to the first man on the bench, a wiry old *campesino*.
I kneel down and wash his feet. It's not as strange a feeling as I thought
it would be—maybe it's in my Benedictine blood? I finish drying his feet
and stand up to move to the next person.

When I glance down the line of twelve people, I blink in surprise. At
the other end of the row, Gertulio is on his knees washing someone's feet,
and in the center Sister Teresa is washing someone else's. "What," I ask
myself, "are these two people up to?" In a second, though, I understand
what's happening. For the past few years there has been no priest here on
Holy Thursday, and the catechist and the sisters, the central figures in this
little faith community, have run the service themselves, including in it the
footwashing ritual. They and their tiny community found it so meaningful

and so beautiful that the two of them just naturally continued the tradition this year.

With three of us involved, the ceremony goes quickly, and soon I'm rinsing my hands and putting on my white chasuble again to continue the rest of the Mass. While a young woman leads the long list of petitions in the "General Intercessions," I notice my two fellow foot-washers in the front row, and I start to think about what the three of us have just done.

When I, the visiting priest, washed the feet of some people, I was "playing Christ" in a ritualized liturgical drama. But Sister Teresa and Gertulio were, it seems to me, doing something else: they were simply obeying Jesus' command, "If I have washed your feet, you should wash one another's." Their ritual gesture of service this evening is just a pale symbol of what they in fact do for people all the time. Gertulio gives himself entirely to evangelizing the poor and helping them solve all sorts of everyday problems. Sister Teresa spends long days distributing medicine at her little dispensary, working with children, comforting the dying, consoling the sorrowful, and bringing the Good News to the poor. These two give their lives for their sisters and brothers by obeying Jesus' "new command" to "love one another just as I have loved you."

What if I had the vision to see each person in my life as someone whose feet I'm supposed to wash? What if my first response at the approach of a student, a brother monk, or a parishioner were always the desire to be of service the way Jesus was?

I'm called back with a jolt as Carlos puts the microphone in front of me. He holds up the Spanish text and I begin to read the oration at the end of the petitions. When the congregation responds "Amen" and we sit down again, I start to look out at all the saints on the benches. Some of them are barefoot, some in shower clogs. Many are wearing T-shirts and cheap cotton shorts. Their clothes tell a tale of poverty. But their faces say something else. Thanks to Gertulio and Sisters Teresa and Ana, these poor people have received a priceless gift: they know that they are loved by God, a God who kneels to serve them—a God who washes their feet.

Reflection

Jesus' journey is about to culminate in a final act of love, when he lays down his life for his friends. John's gospel account of the Last Supper makes no mention of bread or wine or the instituting of the Eucharist; in its place the gospel writer tells the story of Jesus washing the feet of his disciples. The message is clear: sacramental Communion is meaningless without the active life of loving service that it represents.

Has your Lenten journey made you a little more sensitive to each person around you as someone who "needs his or her feet washed?" Think of someone you know who might be especially in need of your loving service.

Sacred Scripture (John 13:3–5, 12–15, RSV)

Jesus, knowing that the Father had given all things into his hands, and that he had come from God and was going to God, rose from supper, laid aside his garments, and girded himself with a towel. Then he poured water into a basin, and began to wash the disciples' feet, and to wipe them with the towel with which he was girded. When he had washed their feet, and taken his garments, and resumed his place, he said to them, "Do you know what I have done to you? You call me Teacher and Lord; and you are right, for so I am. If I then, your Lord and Teacher, have washed your feet, you also ought to wash one another's feet. For I have given you an example, that you also should do as I have done to you."

Rule of Benedict

"The abbot shall pour water on the hands of the guests, and the abbot with the entire community shall wash their feet" (Chapter 53, "The Reception of Guests," vv. 12–13).

"Both the one who is ending his service [in the kitchen] and the one who is about to begin are to be wash the feet of everyone" (Chapter 35, "Kitchen Servers for the Week," v. 9).

Good Friday

Fatima Parish, Santa Cruz:
Waving Your Palm

In the open-air market here in Santa Cruz, in the semi-tropical center of Bolivia, I've seen the dried llama fetuses that one buries in the foundation of a new house to ward off evil. In the center of town, I've marveled at the old women who sit on the sidewalk patiently waiting all day for someone to buy one or two of the oranges they've put on the blanket in front of them. On my long walks from the rectory I've watched shiny new Porsches dodge around burro-powered carts on the highway. A few days ago, on Palm Sunday, I saw little children sitting at the gate of the church-yard selling palms before Mass. Nothing surprises me anymore now that I've been here for over a week.

So I'm not shocked to see a woman show up for the Good Friday service carrying a long ribbon-like piece of last Sunday's palm. Then, as people start filling the pews, I notice more and more of these yellow branches appearing. By the start of the service in honor of the Passion and Death of Our Lord, there are palms in every part of the church.

The liturgy begins in silence with the procession of priests and altar servers. In the sanctuary we four priests quietly prostrate ourselves on the floor for a moment as a sign of repentance. Then we stand and the pastor prays the opening oration. Everyone sits down and the readings begin.

In the deep faith of the *campesinos*, the simple country people, religious practices are sometimes a confused mixture of native religion, superstition, and imperfect Christian theology. But when I look out over the crowded church this Good Friday afternoon, their custom of celebrating "Palm Friday" starts to speak powerfully to me. The pious folks who have come back today carrying last Sunday's palms with them actually show deep insight into the great paradox of Christian life.

The bright yellow strips of palm are accusing fingers pointing to a sad truth: we are the same people who greeted Jesus at his triumphal entrance into Jerusalem just five days ago. We recognized the Messiah and sang out in joy, "Hosanna to the Son of David! Blessed is he who comes in the name of the Lord!" We tore branches off of trees and laid them on the road for his donkey to walk on. But that was Sunday. And this is Friday. Today our hands, the same hands that waved the branches in homage, are clenched fists shaking angrily at the pathetic figure crowned with thorns. The same congregation that was Sunday's welcoming throng has turned into Friday's bloodthirsty mob. The same voices that sang out "Hosanna! Hosanna!" last Sunday are shouting "Crucify him! Crucify him!" this afternoon.

After the readings and prayers comes the ancient ceremony of the veneration of the cross. Worshipers stream single-file toward the crucifix to kiss the image of their Savior. Once again, the accusing palms appear here and there in the line.

We are amazingly fickle creatures when you think about it. We pray, we go to church, and then without a qualm we turn and calmly crucify Christ in our neighbor with a well-aimed insult. We thank God with great fervor for loving us unconditionally, but then a moment later refuse to help a neighbor in need. Palm Sunday turns into Good Friday with alarming speed. No wonder Benedict talks so much about "prayer with tears" and "compunction of heart."

At the end of the service, a procession forms behind a life-size cross that is being carried out of the church and through the streets on a public Way of the Cross. The church empties as the crowd forms a procession to visit fourteen stations that have been placed around the neighborhood. Once again, several yellow palms lift their sharp points upward, looking more and more like accusing fingers all the time as they wave slowly in the wake of the life-size cross.

The palm branches have an interesting role in Holy Week. The saints on earth carry them in the crowd on Palm Sunday as symbols of our belief that Jesus is the Messiah. Some saints carry them in the Good Friday procession as a reminder of our weakness and unfaithfulness. But the palm branches don't disappear with the burial of Jesus. No, they show up one last time at the end of every believer's journey. In the Book of Revelation, Saint John tells us:

> After that I saw that there was a huge number, impossible for anyone to count, of people from every nation, race, tribe and language; they were standing in front of the throne and in front of the Lamb, dressed in white robes and holding palms in their hands. They shouted in a loud voice, "Salvation to our God, who sits on the throne, and to the Lamb!"

In the victory celebration in heaven, all the saints will be carrying palms. The branches will be the sign of our sharing in Christ's final triumph over sin, over our unfaithfulness and over death itself.

The procession has left the church now. A few dozen people have stayed behind to go to confession. I walk over and sit on a hard wooden chair in the little open alcove that will be my confessional. The first penitent, a sun-dried old man, shuffles toward me. A well-worn palm branch is clutched in his gnarled brown hand. Will he bring it with him once again, I wonder, when he comes to celebrate on Easter Sunday?

Reflection

Picture yourself in two different crowds. First, you're standing with hundreds of people lining the road as Jesus enters Jerusalem on Palm Sunday; you're waving a palm branch and shouting "Hosanna!" with everyone around you. Next, you're standing at the foot of the cross on Calvary in the crowd that has called for Jesus' death; in Bolivian style, you're carrying the very same piece of palm you had with you on Sunday.

Do you feel the harsh contrast between the two scenes, and the bitter irony of your situation? When and how do fickleness and unfaithfulness to God tend to play themselves out in your life? Stay on Calvary and pray for a few minutes at the foot of the cross.

If this exercise starts to get too depressing, then try this: picture yourself standing with your piece of palm in the throng of white-robed saints in heaven and shouting with boundless joy, "Salvation to our God, who sits on the throne, and to the Lamb!" The Lamb shed his blood on Calvary for you precisely so that you could stand in this heavenly throng and wave your palm branch and shout in joyful triumph for all eternity. Try making up a prayer of thanks to the crucified Savior.

Sacred Scripture (John 19:14–18, RSV)

[Pilate] said to the Jews, "Behold your King!" They cried out, "Away with him, away with him, crucify him!" Pilate said to them, "Shall I crucify your King?" The chief priests answered, "We have no king but Caesar." Then he handed him over to them to be crucified. So they took Jesus, and he went out, bearing his own cross, to the place called the place of a skull, which is called in Hebrew Golgotha. There they crucified him, and with him two others, one on either side, and Jesus between them.

Rule of Benedict (Chapter 7, "Humility," v. 34)

"The third step of humility is that a man submits to his superior in all obedience for the love of God, imitating the Lord of whom the Apostle says: He became obedient even to death."

Holy Saturday

Saint Martin du Canigou, France:
Waiting in Joyful Hope

The gray peaks of the Pyrenees stretch out in a ragged semi-circle in front of me; their lower slopes, carpeted in lush, dark green, plunge out of sight into steep chasms. A hundred feet below my rocky perch, the tan stone buildings of the Abbey of Saint Martin du Canigou cling precariously to a rocky outcropping. Beside the small church with its squat, square-topped bell tower and gray slate roof, the main two-story monastery basks in the morning sunshine, looking down onto the enclosed cloister garden, with its open colonnade on one side that follows the edge of a steep cliff. At the far end of the garden is another simple two-story stone building; like a few of the others it has a red tile roof. In the wall of its flagstone porch the two red wooden French doors of my room are closed tight against the coming heat.

Although the little monastery which is my home for the week is 3,500 feet above sea level, it is dwarfed on three sides by much higher peaks. I can almost feel the solemn, imposing presence of the majestic 8,500 foot bulk of Mount Canigou, out of sight beyond the shoulder of the ridge to my right.

It's almost time for Midday Prayer in the chapel, so I get up from the boulder that I've been using as a seat, turn around, and start to pick my way carefully down the steep path toward the monastery. It occurs to me that the peaceful scene down there certainly doesn't reflect the trouble and tumult that have marred the abbey's history.

It was founded almost a thousand years ago by a local lord, Guilford Cabreta, with the help of his brother, the abbot of the famous monastery of Saint Michel de Cuxa, some miles distant. Saint Martin's future was to prove neither illustrious nor peaceful. Over the next 700 years it would continually be the target of some sort of intrigue or other involving local Catalan nobles, the powerful Abbot of Ripoll, or some local bishop. Armies would twice make their way up the holy mountain to loot the monastery. In 1428 an earthquake would reduce a number of its walls to rubble.

Thinking about the earthquake reminds me to keep my eyes down and watch my footing—the steep, rocky path roughly resembles a staircase with uneven steps, some of them two feet high.

Rebuilt immediately after the earthquake, the little monastery was still not destined to leave much of a trace on local history during the next 350 years. Finally, in 1783, the five elderly monks who were left decided that they could no longer keep up the monastic life here in "this frightful solitude." So one sad day they closed up the monastery and set off down the mountain, taking with them their most prized possessions, including the monastery's archives and library. The old men and their treasures vanished without a trace.

As soon as the monks abandoned the place, the harsh climate began to take its toll on walls and roofs, and the forest began to reclaim its territory. Local people came up from the valley to help themselves to columns and carved capitals until eventually the entire cloister disappeared. The ruins of Saint Martin du Canigou became just one more romantic picnic spot in the French Pyrenees. Today's neat, well-kept buildings are a clear sign that something unexpected has happened to the romantic ruins.

In the 1920s the newly appointed Bishop of Perpignan, Abbé de Carsalade, who had always been attracted by the mystery of the place, decided that the ruins of Saint Martin's should be restored so that God's praises could once again be sung on the mountain. Thus began an inspiring story of resurrection.

His idea caught on, and with plenty of popular support for the project, the little monastery church was rebuilt, then the guest hostel and two monastery buildings. A quarter of the original stone columns and their capitals were recovered and used in a new cloister garden. Over the years, teams of volunteers have spent every summer rebuilding and repairing Saint Martin's.

Since the simple stone buildings have no heating at all, the place is always closed during the bitter cold winter months. During the summer, the monastery is staffed by volunteers who are led by a couple of monks of L'Haye les Roses near Paris. They welcome the thousands of pilgrims who make the long trek up the mountain road to the monastery. These days the place is able to host up to sixty-four overnight guests at a time.

I join the wide dusty road that leads to the entrance, and step through the simple gate into the cloister garden. In the glaring sunlight I make my way slowly along the flagstones toward the church. Just to the left of the small arched door, I notice one of the more curious features of Saint Martin's: a depression the size of a small bathtub carved into a flat section of the granite mountainside. The volunteer guides love to tell the story of how it got here.

It seems that the abbey's founding patron, Guilford Cabreta, eventually joined the monastery himself and lived out his last fourteen years here as a simple monk. Shortly after his arrival, he asked to have his grave dug right away, near the entrance to the church, to remind him each day of the brevity of life and the futility of all earthly honors. The first time I saw this grave and heard the story I dismissed the whole thing as slightly bizarre, a typical example of medieval religious eccentricity.

The ringing of a high pitched bell in the church tower breaks in on my reflection. Its song rides on the warm breeze across the little ravine to the east, and echoes off of the tan stone cliff, calling our little community of monks, lay volunteers, and visitors to Midday Prayer. I turn and step through the low, rounded arch into the little church; a few others are already kneeling in the quiet shadows.

As I sit in the cool semi-darkness, I can still picture that empty grave outside. Suddenly it strikes me that what's important is not that it's a grave, but that it's *empty*. I hear the deafening blast of a trumpet; before my eyes every grave that ever was bursts open in an instant, in the twinkling of an eye. Every unmarked trench on every battlefield on earth suddenly lies open and empty in the bright sunshine. Every little child's grave, every ditch ever dug in a pauper's field now lies open and empty in the bright sunshine. Every tomb, every burial mound, every mausoleum, suddenly lies open and empty in the bright sunshine. I see the graves of my mother and father, of my sister and brother and of all my relatives, all suddenly lying open and empty in the bright sunshine. And, best of all, I can see my own grave in Saint Mary's Cemetery suddenly lying open and empty in the bright sunshine. . . .

Père Hugues gives the signal to begin, and the voices of twenty men and women fill the chapel with a simple, beautiful song. The monastery of Saint Martin du Canigou, twice sacked by soldiers, racked by an earthquake, lying in ruins and overrun by the forest for years, is alive again; the holy mountain is singing once more.

Outside in the cloister garden is the grave of Guilford de Cabreta, lying open and empty in the bright sunshine.

Reflection

Picture a particular cemetery, and the grave of someone you love. Sit with this image for a few minutes: what sounds do you hear? What do you see? What memories of this person and what feelings does this image evoke? Do you remember the day he or she was buried?

Now imagine that it is the end of time, and that same grave is now lying open and empty in the bright sunshine of eternity. You are reunited with that loved one. What do you say to him or her? What emotions do you feel? Our belief in the Easter mystery includes exactly this scene.

Benedict says, "Day by day remind yourself that you are going to die." Today, on Holy Saturday, as the Church waits longingly for Jesus to rise from the tomb, reflect instead on this statement: "Day by day remind yourself that you are going to *live forever*."

Sacred Scripture (John 19:40–42, RSV)

"They took the body of Jesus, and bound it in linen cloths with the spices, as is the burial custom of the Jews. Now in the place where he was crucified there was a garden, and in the garden a new tomb where no one had ever been laid. So because of the Jewish day of Preparation, as the tomb was close at hand, they laid Jesus there."

Rule of Benedict
(Chapter 4, "The Tools for Good Works," vv. 44, 46–47)

"Live in fear of judgement day. . . . Yearn for everlasting life with holy desire. Day by day remind yourself that you are going to die."

EPILOGUE

We have reached the end of our spiritual travelogue. Remembering that a pilgrimage is supposed to leave you changed forever, look back over the past six and a half weeks and ask yourself if you haven't perhaps seen some changes in yourself. Whether those changes are great or small, you have to celebrate them, nurture them, let them sink into your being and become part of you.

How do you intend to continue responding to the call to conversion tomorrow, and the next day, and the day after that? This question points up a crucial difference between this journey and others. When the catechumens walk in procession to the baptismal font at the Easter Vigil, for example, that marks the end of their journey of preparation. When pilgrims finally arrived at Santiago de Compostela, each one would reverently touch the stone statue of Saint James carved into the center door post of the church, signaling that he or she had finally and officially "arrived."

When we Lenten pilgrims arrive at Easter Sunday, then, we are naturally tempted to think that we, like catechumens or medieval pilgrims, have reached the end of our journey. But this is not the case. We all remain constant catechumens, perpetual pilgrims always on the road. A fellow Benedictine, Father Demetrius Dumm, puts it this way:

> In God's loving plan, the victory was never meant to take place here, much as we would like that to happen. Thus we must endure the painful twinges that are inevitable for those who are on a journey. Legitimate but provisional attachments must give way to permit the only attachment that will never need to be broken—our attachment to the Father in Jesus and the Spirit. We will know then that this world, though a wonderful place to visit, was never

meant to be our real home. The Spirit helps us to understand this as he creates in us a kind of homesickness—an aching void—that can never be filled with anything less than God.[6]

Any of the forty meditations in this book can be used appropriately at any time of year. Put this pilgrim journal on a shelf where you can see it, and go back and reread a chapter whenever the Spirit moves you. Its pages will speak to you again in that new place on your journey, perhaps with even more effect than they did when you first read them.

Let us end this book as we began it, with a prayer for God's protection and guidance. This beautiful ancient blessing for pilgrims setting off for Compostela makes a fitting final prayer for all of us as we continue along life's Pilgrim Road:

O God, who led your servant Abraham from the city of Ur, guarding him through all his pilgrimage, and you who were the guide of the Hebrew people through the desert, we ask you to protect these your servants who, for the love of your name, journey to Compostela. Be for them a companion on the march, a guide at the crossroads; give them strength when they are weak, defense in the midst of danger, shelter along the route, shade from the sun, light in the darkness, solace in moments of discouragement and firmness in their purpose. . . . May the blessing of God the All-Powerful, Father, Son, and Holy Spirit, descend upon you. Amen.[7]

---

6. Demetrius Dumm, O.S.B., *A Mystical Portrait of Jesus* (Collegeville, Minn.: Liturgical Press, 2001), 64–65.

7. Nicholas Shrady, *Sacred Roads: Adventures from the Pilgrimage Trail* (San Francisco: HarperSanFrancisco, 1999), 160.